36

Great Regional Food Made Simple

John Topham

LAMONA & John Topham

The Perfect Combination

HOWDENS
JOINERY CO.

MAKING SPACE MORE VALUABLE

John Topham

Great Regional Food Made Simple

We're so lucky in the UK to have such a wide variety of fantastic food throughout our regions. From Scottish shortbread to Dover sole, a wealth of traditional dishes have become part of our culture. And we're constantly seeing new recipes, created by today's chefs looking for exciting ways to use local produce.

There's so much to try – and more to discover – that I decided to embark on a gastronomic journey, exploring the food in eight of our fascinating regions. I tasted black pudding in Lancashire, blue cheese in Dorset, and lots more in between. Along the way, I called in at some outstanding local inns, to check out the menu and see where they buy their wonderful ingredients.

Then it was back to my kitchen, armed with information and inspiration, to create the recipes collected here. I've also included dishes from the inns I visited. I've tested them on Lamona appliances, so I'm confident the results will be delicious – whether you're a keen chef or new to cooking.

Whatever shape and size your kitchen, the Lamona range offers all the choice and versatility you need. I'm very happy to recommend these appliances – especially when it comes to trying these great regional recipes!

John Topham

Head Chef and owner, The General Tarleton

LAMONA & John Topham
The Perfect Combination

The General Tarleton

03

REGIONS

The Bull, Great Totham

EAST ANGLIA

Including Norfolk, Suffolk, Cambridgeshire and Essex, East Anglia contains more than half of the most productive agricultural land in England and Wales. The wide variety of farming here makes it a marvellous place for food — whether it's poultry, pigs or parsnips! Also, with miles of coastline, there's plenty of fish and seafood.

So I wasn't surprised to find that The Bull in Great Totham, Essex, prides itself on sourcing ingredients as locally as possible for its award-winning restaurant. Meat is a big feature on the menu, supplied by a producer in a nearby village, and I thoroughly enjoyed tasting the superb quality.

With an equally strong emphasis on fruit and dairy farming, desserts are also extremely popular in the region. You'll see some tempting examples here, along with savoury dishes designed to show off East Anglia's best produce.

EAST ANGLIA RECIPES

Baked Cromer Crab

Baked Cromer Crab

Cromer is famous for its sweet-tasting crabs, and this recipe brings out the best in them. Using the shells for presentation, it makes an impressive starter or lunch.

Serves 4 15 mins preparation, 15 mins cooking

Ingredients

4 shallots, peeled and finely diced
2 cloves garlic, crushed
2 sticks celery, peeled and finely diced
50g unsalted butter
50ml dry sherry
4 medium dressed crabs (in their shells)
1 dessertspoon English mustard
Large pinch nutmeg

2 tablespoons parsley, chopped
Juice of ½ lemon
4 tablespoons breadcrumbs
Sea salt and milled black pepper
100g Cheddar cheese, grated

To serve
Warm toast

1. Pre-heat the grill to high.

2. In a large frying pan, gently cook the shallots, garlic and celery in 25g of the butter until softened. Pour in the sherry and bring to a simmer.

3. Carefully scoop the crabmeat out of the shells into the pan, keeping the shells to one side. Add the mustard and nutmeg, warm through for 5 minutes.

4. Remove the pan from the heat, and stir in the parsley, lemon juice and half of the breadcrumbs. Season with salt and pepper.

5. Spoon the mixture back into the crab shells, sprinkle with the cheese and remaining breadcrumbs. Place a few dots of butter on each one, and place under the grill for 2-3 minutes until golden. Serve with warm toast.

Curried Parsnip Soup

Parsnips are a very British vegetable, and East Anglia is an important growing area for them. A hint of curry enhances their slightly sweet flavour in this wholesome, hearty soup.

Serves 4-6 10 mins preparation, 30 mins cooking

Ingredients
30g unsalted butter
1 onion, peeled and chopped
4 parsnips, peeled and evenly chopped
½ bulb fennel, chopped
1 stick celery, chopped
1 large potato, peeled and chopped
1 dessertspoon medium curry powder
1 litre vegetable stock
1 teaspoon cumin seeds
4 tablespoons crème fraîche
Sea salt and milled black pepper

1. Melt the butter in a large pan over a medium heat. Then add the onion and parsnips, and stir for 2 minutes before reducing the heat. Put a lid on the pan, and cook very gently for 5 minutes.

2. Add the fennel, celery and potato, along with the curry powder, and cook for a further 2 minutes before adding the vegetable stock. Bring to the boil, reduce the heat to a simmer and cook for another 20 minutes.

3. Heat a small frying pan, add the cumin seeds and dry fry for 2 minutes. Put them in a pestle and mortar, and grind to a powder.

4. Mix the cumin with the crème fraîche, and keep to one side.

5. Pour the soup into a blender, and blitz until smooth. Check the seasoning, adding salt and pepper if necessary, and pour into soup bowls. Serve with a swirl of the cumin crème fraîche.

Curried Parsnip Soup

Creamed Ported Stilton with Poached Pears, Beetroot, Hazelnuts and Watercress

Creamed Ported Stilton with Poached Pears, Beetroot, Hazelnuts and Watercress

Originating in the village of Stilton, Cambridgeshire, Stilton cheese has a saltiness that works brilliantly with the sweetness of port and poached pears. Here, beetroot, hazelnuts and watercress add further flavour and texture to make a wonderful starter or light lunch.

Serves 4 40 mins preparation

Ingredients

2 pears
250ml white wine
2 tablespoons clear honey
300g Stilton cheese
50ml port
100ml double cream

2 bunches watercress
4 baby beetroot, cooked
100g hazelnuts, roasted and lightly crushed
Milled black pepper
1 lemon
3 tablespoons rapeseed oil

1. Peel the pears and put in a saucepan with the white wine and honey. Add enough cold water to cover the pears. Bring this to the boil, then reduce the heat to a gentle simmer and cook for 10-20 minutes, until the pears are tender. Leave to cool.

2. While the pears are cooling, place the Stilton, port and double cream in a large bowl. Using your hands, cream together until combined (you'll need to squeeze them through your fingers). Keep the mixture in the fridge until you need it.

3. Slice the beetroot and the cooled pears, and arrange them on 4 serving plates. Pick through the watercress and place on the plates.

4. Using 2 tablespoons, scoop a quarter of the Stilton mixture from one spoon to another, shaping it as you go until you have a smooth, oval shape, or 'quenelle'. Repeat this to make 4, and place each one in the centre of the salad. Scatter each plate with hazelnuts, then finish with a grind of pepper, a squeeze of lemon juice and a drizzle of rapeseed oil.

Roast Goose, Sage and Onion Stuffing, and Apple Sauce

18

Roast Goose, Sage and Onion Stuffing, and Apple Sauce

Geese are a big part of farming in East Anglia. They produce a rich, tasty meat that deserves more attention across the country – as you'll discover when you try this delicious roast.

Serves 8 45 mins preparation, 2 hours to 2 hours 30 mins cooking

Ingredients
1 goose with giblets (4-5kg)
Sea salt and milled black pepper
1 onion, peeled and roughly chopped
2 sticks celery, roughly chopped
1 carrot, peeled and roughly chopped
2 bay leaves
1 sprig thyme
1 litre chicken stock

For the apple sauce
4 Bramley apples, peeled, cored and sliced
1 tablespoon caster sugar
1 tablespoon water

For the stuffing
2 large onions, finely chopped
75g butter
Zest of 1 lemon
4 tablespoons fresh sage, chopped
3 tablespoons fresh parsley, chopped
1 tablespoon picked fresh thyme leaves
350g breadcrumbs
Sea salt and milled black pepper
1 egg, lightly beaten

To serve
Watercress

Roasting tin
Wire rack

1. Pre-heat the oven to 220°C/gas mark 7.

2. Remove any excess fat from the goose and reserve the giblets. Place the goose on wire rack in an empty sink. Boil a kettle of water and pour all over the goose. Leave to dry.

3. To make the stuffing, fry the onions in the butter until they become soft. Take them off the heat and stir in the lemon zest, herbs and breadcrumbs, and season with salt and pepper. Now add enough beaten egg to bind the mixture together.

Continued on page 20

4. Wipe the cavity of the goose with paper towels, season with a little salt and pepper and fill the cavity with the stuffing. Seal the opening with a skewer.

5. Place the goose on a wire rack in a large roasting tin, and roast for 30 minutes.

6. Remove the tin from the oven. Carefully pour off any excess fat and retain if needed – it's great for making roast potatoes.

7. Turn the oven down to 180°C/gas mark 4. Put the goose back in the oven for a further 1½ to 2 hours, basting it and pouring off the excess fat every 30 minutes.

8. In the meantime, make the gravy by frying the giblets, onion, celery and carrot in a little oil until golden brown. Add the bay leaves, thyme and chicken stock, bring to the boil and simmer for 1 hour. Strain the gravy through a fine sieve, return it to the pan, bring to the boil and reduce the volume by half.

9. When the goose has finished cooking, use a skewer to pierce the thigh and check the juices run clear. (If they don't, the meat will be fine to eat but may be a little pink, so you might want to continue cooking.)

10. Place the goose on a suitable dish, cover it with kitchen foil and keep in a warm place while you finish the gravy.

11. Remove any remaining excess fat from the roasting tin, pour in the giblet gravy and bring it to a simmer. Use a wooden spoon to loosen the baked-on pan juices, then pass the gravy through a sieve into a saucepan and simmer over a low heat until you have a smooth sauce.

To make the apple sauce

1. Put the apples, sugar and water in a saucepan. Cover with a lid and simmer gently for 10 minutes, stirring occasionally until the apples have softened.

To serve

1. Carve the goose and serve with the apple sauce, stuffing, gravy and fresh watercress.

Pan-fried Pork Tenderloin with Caramelised Apple, and Lemon and Caper Butter

This pork recipe from The Bull combines the classic apple accompaniment with thyme, garlic and a tangy lemon and caper butter – perfect flavours to balance the richness of the meat.

Serves 2 30 mins preparation, 30 mins cooking

Ingredients

1 pork tenderloin	1 Gala apple
Sea salt and milled black pepper	½ onion, chopped
2 tablespoons olive oil	100g peas, blanched
30g butter	100g broad beans, blanched and shelled
3 sprigs thyme	Zest of 1 lemon
1 garlic clove, peeled and crushed	1 tablespoon capers
1 tablespoon dark brown sugar	1 tablespoon parsley, chopped

1. Pre-heat a small frying pan.

2. Clean the pork tenderloin by removing fat and connective tissue. Season it generously with salt and pepper, and brush with 1 tablespoon of olive oil. Place in the hot frying pan, and colour it well on all sides.

3. Turn the heat down to low, and add half the butter to the pan, followed by the thyme and garlic. Turn the pork every 5 minutes – do this 4 times, until it's cooked (very slightly pink is perfect).

4. Transfer the pork to a warm plate, cover with foil and leave to rest.

5. Turn up the heat again under the pan, and add the dark brown sugar. While it's caramelising, core the apple and cut into wedges. Add the apple to the caramel and cook slowly. When it starts to break down on the outside, remove from the pan and keep warm.

6. Heat a small saucepan, add the onion and fry in 1 tablespoon of olive oil. Add the remaining butter, then the peas and broad beans, followed by the lemon zest and capers. When everything's hot, season with salt and pepper, and finish with the chopped parsley.

7. Carve the tenderloin into slices, and serve with the apple pieces. Spoon the peas and broad beans generously around the pork, making sure you coat it well in the butter.

Pan-fried Pork Tenderloin with Caramelised Apple, and Lemon and Caper Butter

Trinity Pudding

This luxuriously creamy dessert takes its name from Trinity College, Cambridge, where a student offered the recipe to the college kitchens in the 1860s. Today it goes more often by the French name, crème brûlée – but I want to reassert its English heritage!

Serves 8 15 mins preparation, 10 mins cooking, 4 hours chilling

Ingredients
850ml double cream
1 vanilla pod
7 large egg yolks
25g caster sugar
75g caster sugar for the topping

8 ramekin dishes

1. Pour the cream into a large pan. Split the vanilla pod and scrape the seeds into the cream. Heat slowly, until it's almost boiling.

2. In a bowl, beat the egg yolks and add 25g of caster sugar.

3. When the cream is hot, pour half of it onto the egg yolk mixture and stir well, using a whisk.

4. Pour the cream and egg mixture back into the pan with the rest of the cream, and stir continuously over a low heat until it has a thick, pouring consistency. Do not let it boil.

5. Divide the mixture between 8 ramekin dishes. Let it cool slightly, then put the puddings in the fridge to set for at least 4 hours.

6. Take the puddings out of the fridge. Sprinkle them evenly with the remaining sugar, and then caramelise the surface of each one with a blowtorch or under a hot grill.

Trinity Pudding

Norfolk Treacle Tart

Serves 6-8 35 mins preparation, 1 hour cooking,
1 hour chilling, 2 hours resting

Ingredients

For the pastry
230g plain flour
85g icing sugar
125g chilled unsalted butter, diced
Zest of ½ lemon
1 large egg yolk, lightly beaten
1 egg yolk to seal the pastry

For the filling
60g unsalted butter
450g golden syrup
165ml double cream
75g ground almonds
120g breadcrumbs
1 egg and 1 egg yolk, lightly beaten together
1 teaspoon ground ginger
1 pinch salt
Zest of 1 lemon

To serve
Double cream

25cm tart ring, 3½cm deep, greased
Baking beans or dry rice

To make the pastry

1. Put the flour, icing sugar, butter and lemon zest into a bowl. Using your fingertips, mix together until you have a crumb-like consistency. Slowly mix in the egg yolk to form a dough.

2. Shape the dough into a ball, wrap tightly in cling film and chill in the fridge for an hour.

3. Pre-heat the oven to 180°C/gas mark 4.

4. Line a baking sheet with baking parchment.

5. Lightly dust a work surface with flour, and roll out the pastry until it's 2mm thick. Then use to line the tart ring, letting the excess pastry hang over the sides.

6. Put the ring onto the baking sheet, cover it with baking parchment and cover the base with baking beans or dry rice. Bake the pastry for 15 minutes, until it's lightly coloured.

7. Remove the baking beans and baking parchment, and brush the pastry case with egg yolk. Put it back in the oven to bake for a further 5 minutes.

To make the filling and finish the tart

1. In a saucepan, melt the butter until it foams and has a nut-brown colour.

2. Take the pan off the heat, and add the golden syrup and cream. Mix these together and stir in the rest of the filling ingredients.

3. Pour the mixture into the tart case, and cook in the oven for 25 minutes.

4. Turn the heat down to 140°C/gas mark 1 and cook for a further 15 minutes. Take the tart out of the oven and leave it to cool to room temperature.

5. Trim off the excess pastry, remove the ring and cut the tart into slices. Serve with a good dollop of double cream.

Norfolk Treacle Tart

The Punch Bowl, Crosthwaite

NORTH WEST

Probably one of the UK's most diverse regions, the North West takes in the lakes and mountains of Cumbria, the spectacular Lancashire coastline, and a vibrant mix of market towns and industrial cities. And this means an equally varied choice of food – especially the fresh shellfish, and the succulent meat from livestock grazing in this dramatic green landscape.

My travels took me to The Punch Bowl Inn, in the unspoilt Lyth Valley in Cumbria. Its menu features the best local, seasonal ingredients – including damsons grown in the valley and meat from Udale Speciality Foods, who are renowned in the Lake District and supply some of the best London restaurants.

Chatting to manager Lorraine Stanton and head chef Scott Fairweather, I got really excited about this region's outstanding produce and the creative ways we can cook with it – as I hope you'll see in the recipes over the next few pages.

NORTH WEST RECIPES

Black Pudding, Seared Scallops and Creamed Leeks

Black Pudding, Seared Scallops and Creamed Leeks

Fleetwood in Lancashire is renowned for its shellfish, and black pudding is even more famous in the region. So this is a popular local combination – and here, chicken mousse and Parma ham add to the rich, hearty flavours.

Serves 4 30 mins preparation, 12 mins cooking, 1 hour chilling

Ingredients

1 skinless chicken breast, diced
1 egg
Sea salt and milled black pepper
250ml double cream
3 slices Parma ham
200g piece of black pudding
100ml balsamic vinegar
100g palm sugar

2 medium leeks, washed and finely shredded
45g unsalted butter
2 tablespoons olive oil
12 large fresh king scallops, cleaned and the roe removed
Juice of ½ lemon

Food processor

1. Place the chicken in a food processor and pulse into a smooth paste. Add the egg, season with salt and pepper, and blend until smooth. Slowly pulse in 200ml of cream, a little at a time, creating a smooth mousse. Put into a bowl and keep in the fridge until needed.

2. Spread a large double layer of cling film onto a work surface, and lay Parma ham slices alongside each other, with the edges overlapping slightly. Use a pallet knife to spread the chicken mousse all over the Parma ham slices. Then place the black pudding down one side and roll the ham around it so it overlaps. Roll the cling film tightly around the sausage shape you've created, tie both ends firmly and chill in the fridge for at least an hour.

3. In a small saucepan, bring the balsamic vinegar and palm sugar to the boil, and let them reduce to a sticky sauce. Put to one side to cool.

4. Gently fry the leeks with 25g of the butter, until they're just becoming soft. Add the remaining 50ml of double cream, season with salt and pepper, and simmer gently until the cream thickens slightly.

5. Unwrap the black pudding sausage from the cling film and slice it into 12 pieces. Heat 1 tablespoon of olive oil in a large frying pan, and fry the sliced pudding for 2 minutes on each side. Then transfer it to a dish to keep warm.

6. Clean the frying pan, then heat the remaining tablespoon of olive oil and 20g of butter. When this is foaming, add the king scallops and sear them until golden (2-3 minutes on each side). Season with salt, pepper and a squeeze of lemon.

7. To serve, divide the creamed leeks between 4 plates. Place 3 scallops on each plate, then 3 slices of black pudding, drizzling them with the palm sugar dressing.

Breaded Scampi and Tartare Sauce

Breaded Scampi and Tartare Sauce

Scampi is the culinary name for langoustines, a type of succulent white shellfish related to the lobster. They're caught in the North Atlantic, so they're often at their freshest in the North West – and deep-frying them quickly in breadcrumbs is the best way to capture this freshness.

Serves 4   20 mins preparation, 10 mins cooking

Ingredients
3.5kg beef dripping or 2 litres rapeseed oil
28 fresh langoustines, shelled
100g plain flour
Sea salt and milled black pepper
120g dried breadcrumbs
1 lemon, cut into wedges

For the batter
300g plain flour
250ml beer
1 teaspoon dried yeast
1 egg yolk
Sea salt and milled black pepper

For the tartare sauce
200ml mayonnaise
1 small shallot, finely diced
50g capers
50g gherkins, finely chopped
1 tablespoon parsley, chopped
Juice of ½ lemon
Sea salt and milled black pepper

To serve
Thrice-cooked chips
(see page 62 for my recipe)

Large pan or fryer
Food thermometer

To make the tartare sauce
1. Simply combine all the ingredients in a bowl. Check the seasoning and keep the sauce in the fridge until you need it.

To make the batter
1. In a large bowl, whisk all the ingredients until you have a smooth batter. Keep this to one side in a warm place.

To cook the scampi and serve
1. In an electric deep fryer or large pan, heat the beef dripping or rapeseed oil to 170°C.

2. In batches, dust the langoustines in seasoned flour, dip them into the batter and roll them in breadcrumbs, then put to one side.

3. When the oil is hot enough, carefully cook the langoustines in batches for 4-5 minutes.

4. When they're golden, drain them on kitchen paper. Season with a little salt and serve with the tartare sauce, lemon wedges and thrice-cooked chips.

Cumberland Sausage and Mash with Red Onion Gravy

There's more to this recipe than simple sausage and mash. By using a garlic marinade and cooking these famous regional sausages in the rich, meaty gravy, you get a seriously tasty dish. The humble banger will never be the same again!

Serves 4 20 mins preparation, 1 hour 20 mins cooking, 2-12 hours marinating

Ingredients
1 large ring of Cumberland sausage or
8 large pork sausages

For the marinade
2 tablespoons olive oil
1 large sprig thyme leaves, picked
2 garlic cloves, chopped

For the creamed mashed potatoes
900g King Edward or good mashing
potatoes, peeled and evenly chopped
1 good pinch salt
50g unsalted butter
30ml double cream

For the onion gravy
2 tablespoons olive oil
6 red onions, peeled and sliced
2 cloves garlic, crushed
Sea salt and milled black pepper
250ml red wine
2 bay leaves
500ml beef stock
2 sprigs thyme leaves, picked

1. Put the sausage ring and the marinade ingredients in a large freezer bag. Seal the bag, shake well, and chill in the fridge for at least 2 hours or overnight.

2. Place a large non-stick frying pan over a medium heat. When hot, tip in the contents of the freezer bag and fry for 10-15 minutes, until the sausage is golden brown on all sides. Remove from the pan and keep to one side.

3. Return the pan to the heat, and add the olive oil, onions and garlic. Stir well and season with a little salt and pepper. Cook for 12-15 minutes, stirring occasionally until the onions start to caramelise.

Continued on page 38

Cumberland Sausage and Mash with Red Onion Gravy

4. Pour in the red wine and add the bay leaves. Bring to the boil, and cook for about 10 minutes until the wine has reduced and the onions are soft and gooey.

5. Add the beef stock, mix well and bring back to the boil. Simmer for a further 10 minutes.

6. Return the sausages to the pan and cover with a lid. Reduce the heat to a gentle simmer and cook for 30 minutes.

7. Meanwhile, make the mash. Place the potatoes in a large pan, cover with water and add a good pinch of salt. Bring them to the boil and simmer until soft. Mash them or use a potato ricer, then add the butter and double cream, check the seasoning and beat until smooth.

8. When the sausages are ready, remove them from the heat and keep in a warm place.

9. Add the thyme to the gravy, stir and reduce it if necessary to achieve a sticky consistency.

10. Pour the onion gravy over the sausages and serve with the creamed mashed potatoes.

Slow-Cooked Honey-Glazed Duck

Duck is a particular favourite of mine, especially since I've found an excellent supplier in the North West. This recipe makes the most of its intense flavour and moist texture – and creates amazingly crispy skin.

Serves 4 10 mins preparation, 2 hours 30 mins cooking

Ingredients
1.5kg oven-ready duck
1 tablespoon sea salt
1 dessertspoon cracked white peppercorns
6 heaped tablespoons clear honey

To serve
Creamed mashed potatoes
(see page 36 for my recipe)
Seasonal greens

Roasting tin

1. Pre-heat the oven to 160°C/gas mark 3.

2. Score the duck skin by criss-crossing it lightly with the point of a very sharp knife.

3. Place a wire rack in the base of your kitchen sink, put the duck on top and carefully pour a kettle of boiling water all over it (this helps loosen the fat from the skin to make it crisp). Leave it to dry for 10 minutes, then sprinkle with the salt and cracked peppercorns, rubbing them into the skin.

4. Place the duck in a roasting tin, spoon the honey over it, and put in the oven.

5. After 30 minutes, baste the duck with the honey and duck juices from the bottom of the roasting tin, and then cook for a further 30 minutes. After this, there will be quite a lot of duck fat in the roasting tin, so put the duck on a plate while you tilt the tin and pour off the excess fat into a bowl, leaving the honey in the roasting tin. (Keep the duck fat in the fridge and use it for roast potatoes on another day.)

6. Put the duck back into the roasting tin, baste it with the honey and return to the oven. Slow roast for a further hour, basting every 15 minutes.

7. Remove the excess fat again as before. Then baste the duck with the honey, and return to the oven for the final 30 minutes, basting every 10 minutes. The duck should now be very glazed and sticky.

8. Carve the duck, and serve with creamed mashed potatoes and seasonal greens.

Slow-Cooked Honey-Glazed Duck

Apple and Lyth Valley Damson Custard Pie

Apple and Lyth Valley Damson Custard Pie

In Cumbria's Lyth Valley, The Punch Bowl Inn makes the most of the local damsons, which have a lovely deep flavour when cooked. Their recipe adds custard, apple and an almond-and-rum pastry – and you can make it as individual desserts in jars.

Serves 6-8 1 hour 30 mins preparation, 10 mins cooking, 1 hour chilling

Ingredients

For the pastry
120g softened unsalted butter
200g caster sugar
2 eggs
4 tablespoons dark rum
250g plain flour
2 teaspoons baking powder
50g ground almonds

For the damson purée
1kg damsons (preferably from the Lyth Valley)
500g caster sugar
250g water

For the custard
1 litre semi-skimmed milk
1 vanilla pod, split lengthways
8 egg yolks
150g caster sugar
100g cornflour
250g of the damson purée

For the apple compote
4 Bramley apples
50ml water
100g caster sugar

Food processor
8 ovenproof serving jars
Piping bag

To make the pastry

1. Mix together the butter and sugar until pale and creamy.

2. Stir in the eggs gradually, one at a time, followed by the dark rum.

3. Sift together the flour and baking powder, and fold them carefully into the mixture, along with the ground almonds. Keep folding until they're fully incorporated, but be careful not to overwork the pastry.

4. Wrap the pastry in cling film and chill in the fridge for 1 hour.

Continued on page 44

To make the damson purée

1. Place all the ingredients in a heavy-bottomed saucepan over a high heat, boil them until the damsons have softened and the liquid has reduced to a light syrup consistency.

2. Remove the stones, then transfer the liquid to a food processor. Blitz to a purée, then pass through a fine sieve.

To make the custard

1. Bring the milk and vanilla pod to the boil in a heavy-bottomed saucepan. Remove from the heat, and let them infuse for 5 minutes before removing the vanilla pod.

2. Whisk together the egg yolks, sugar and cornflour, until pale and thickened, and then pour them into the warm milk.

3. Put the pan over a low heat, and whisk the mixture continuously until it's thick enough to coat the back of a spoon. Pass it through a fine sieve, and then stir in the damson purée.

4. Store the custard in the fridge until you need it. It will keep for up to 3 days.

To make the apple compote

1. Peel, core and chop the apples into 1cm cubes. Place them in a saucepan with the water and sugar, and cook gently over a medium heat until the apples are tender but still keep their shape – check this with the point of a sharp knife.

2. Remove the compote from the heat and transfer to 8 ovenproof serving jars. Store in the fridge until you need it. It will keep for up to 3 days.

To assemble and cook the dish

1. Pre-heat the oven to 180°C/gas mark 4.

2. Using a piping bag, pipe the custard on top of the compote in the ovenproof serving jars.

3. Roll out the pastry until it's ½cm thick, then use a suitable pastry cutter to cut out 8 small circles the same size as your jars.

4. Lay the pastry on top of the custard and push it down gently around the edges. Use a metal skewer to pierce several steaming holes in the top, and then bake for 8-10 minutes until the pastry is golden.

5. Serve warm or cold.

Sticky Toffee Pudding

Sticky Toffee Pudding

Several regions claim to have invented this hugely popular dessert, but the most reliable story is that Francis Coulson of the Sharrow Bay hotel in the Lake District developed the recipe we enjoy today. Moist, comforting and wickedly sweet, it's pure indulgence on a plate.

Serves 6-8 15 mins preparation, 40 mins cooking

Ingredients
100g butter, plus 20g extra to grease the dish
350g caster sugar, plus 20g extra to dust the dish
2 eggs, beaten
450g self-raising flour
2 teaspoons baking powder
350g dates, chopped
2 teaspoons bicarbonate of soda
570ml boiling water

For the caramel sauce
200g butter
200g brown sugar
200ml double cream

To serve
Ice cream or double cream

Baking tray

1. Pre-heat the oven to 180°C/gas mark 4.

2. Mix the butter and sugar together, then add the eggs gradually, beating well after each addition. Fold in the flour and baking powder.

3. Prepare a deep-sided baking tray by greasing it with the extra butter and then dusting with the extra sugar, covering it evenly.

4. Put the dates and bicarbonate of soda in a bowl, pour the boiling water over, and mix together. Add this to the other mixed ingredients and fold in.

5. Pour the pudding mixture into the baking tray and bake in the oven for 40 minutes.

To make the caramel sauce
1. Heat the butter, sugar and cream gently in a pan, until the sugar has dissolved.

To finish and serve the pudding
1. When the pudding is ready, take it out of the oven and, while it's still hot, prick the surface with a fork and pour the caramel sauce over.

2. Serve with ice cream or double cream.

Eccles Cakes

No one knows who invented these flaky, buttery, currant-filled cakes, but they were first sold in the town of Eccles, Greater Manchester, in the late 18th century. They've retained their popularity ever since – and you'll see why when you try this recipe.

Makes 10 30 mins preparation, 30 mins cooking, 2 hours 20 mins chilling

Ingredients
For the pastry
175g unsalted butter
225g plain flour
2 tablespoons cold water

For the glaze
1 egg white, beaten
1 tablespoon caster sugar

10cm round cutter
Parchment-lined baking sheet

For the filling
25g unsalted butter
150g currants
50g sultanas
75g soft brown sugar
Zest of 1 lemon
Zest of 1 orange
1 tablespoon orange juice
1 pinch nutmeg
1 pinch ground cinnamon

To make the pastry
1. Before you start, chill the butter in the freezer for an hour.

2. Sift the flour into a large bowl, and grate the chilled butter over it, using a coarse grater. Add the cold water and, using a table knife, mix the ingredients to form a dough.

3. Wrap the dough in cling film and chill in the fridge for an hour.

To make the filling and cook the cakes
1. Put all the filling ingredients into a pan and cook them gently for 5 minutes. Allow them to cool.

2. Roll out the pastry until it's 3mm thick, and cut out 10 discs using a 10cm round cutter.

3. Brush the edge of each disc with a little water, and place 2 heaped teaspoons of filling in the middle of each one. Then lift the edges upwards and pinch them together, sealing them over the filling. Turn the cakes over and pat down to flatten them until the mixture is visible through the pastry.

4. Put them on a parchment-lined baking sheet, and chill in the fridge for 20 minutes.

5. Pre-heat the oven to 180°C/gas mark 4.

6. Brush the top of each cake lightly with the beaten egg white. Cut 3 small slashes across each one and sprinkle with caster sugar. Bake the cakes for 25-30 minutes, until golden brown. Serve warm or at room temperature.

The Oak Tree, Hutton Magna

NORTH EAST

When you consider how everyone moves around, it's amazing we still have so many regional dishes. The North East probably has more than its fair share, as it includes not only Northumberland – with such traditional recipes as Pan Haggerty and Singin' Hinnies – but also Yorkshire, with its Wensleydale cheese, York hams and, of course, Yorkshire pudding.

My stopover in this region was The Oak Tree Inn, in Hutton Magna, on the North Yorkshire and County Durham border. The kitchen creates unusual combinations of local produce – helped by suppliers such as Martin Walker, who delivers vegetables to the inn on his tractor.

In this section, I've put together some of the most distinctive recipes of both Northumberland and Yorkshire. Wherever you live in the country, I'm sure these northern flavours will go down well.

NORTH EAST RECIPES

Fillet of Scarborough Cod with Aubergine Purée, Pink Fir Apple Potatoes and Green Olive Dressing

Creative fish dishes are always on the menu at The Oak Tree Inn, and this recipe enhances a simple piece of cod with a variety of interesting flavours – not least the creamy, nutty Pink Fir Apple variety of potato.

Serves 4 20 mins preparation, 10 mins cooking

Ingredients
4 large Pink Fir Apple potatoes
Sea salt and milled black pepper
30ml olive oil
50g unsalted butter
2 x 8oz cod portions
Squeeze of lemon juice

For the olive dressing
8 green olives, stoned and chopped
1 shallot, peeled and diced
½ teaspoon Dijon mustard
100ml Virgin olive oil
Juice of ¼ lemon

For the aubergine purée
1 teaspoon fennel seeds
100ml olive oil
Pinch sea salt
2 shallots, peeled and sliced
1 garlic clove, peeled and sliced
2 aubergines, peeled and diced

To serve
Spinach

Food processor

1. Boil the potatoes. When they've cooled down a little, carefully peel off the skin.
2. Slice, season with salt and keep warm.

To make the aubergine purée
1. Toast the fennel seeds in a hot pan, then add the olive oil, salt, shallots and garlic.
2. Cook until the shallots and garlic become soft, but don't let them colour.
3. Add the aubergines, cover with a lid and cook on a low heat until soft.
4. Place the mixture in a food processor, purée and pass through a sieve. Keep warm.

To make the olive dressing
1. Mix all the ingredients together and season to taste.

To cook the cod and finish the dish
1. Put the oil and butter in a frying pan, and fry the cod for 3 minutes on each side.
2. Remove from the pan. Season with salt and pepper and add a squeeze of lemon.
3. Serve on a warm plate with the olive dressing, aubergine purée and slices of potato on a bed of spinach.

Fillet of Scarborough Cod with Aubergine Purée, Pink Fir Apple Potatoes and Green Olive Dressing

Pan Haggerty

Pan Haggerty

Filling and wholesome, this traditional Northumbrian dish is a wonderful way to cook potatoes, said to have taken its name from the french 'Hacher', meaning to chop or slice. I serve it here with crème fraîche and a salad.

Serves 4 15 mins preparation, 40 mins cooking

Ingredients
40g butter
1 tablespoon rapeseed oil
150g Cheddar cheese, grated (set aside 50g to grill)
500g Desiree potatoes, peeled and thinly sliced
2 onions, peeled and thinly sliced
Sea salt and milled black pepper

To serve
Mixed leaf salad
Crème fraîche

1. In a large, heavy-based pan, heat the butter and rapeseed oil. Then take it off the heat and swirl the butter and oil around to cover the sides of the pan.

2. Place a layer of potatoes in the bottom of the pan, followed by a layer of onions and then cheese. Season between each layer, and repeat until you've used all the potatoes and onions.

3. Place the pan over a low heat, cover with a lid and cook gently for 30 minutes, until the potatoes are tender.

4. Turn up the heat to brown and crisp the potatoes.

5. Pre-heat the grill to moderate. Sprinkle the remaining cheese over the potatoes and grill the Pan Haggerty until it's golden and bubbling.

6. Cut it into wedges and serve hot with the mixed leaf salad and crème fraîche.

Pressed York Ham Terrine and Pease Pudding

Pressed York Ham Terrine and Pease Pudding

Yorkshire is famous for its pig farming and York hams. Here we make the slow-cooked meat into a tender terrine, to enjoy with pease pudding, a classic of the North East.

Serves 8 40 mins preparation, 4 hours cooking, chill overnight

Ingredients
3 ham shanks, covered with water and soaked overnight
1 pig's trotter
1 onion, peeled
2 carrots, peeled
1 stick celery
2 bay leaves
4 black peppercorns
2 cloves
2 tablespoons red wine vinegar
1 large bunch of flat leaf parsley, stalks separated from the leaves

For the pease pudding
350g yellow split peas, soaked overnight
1 pinch sea salt
45ml cider vinegar
100ml walnut oil

To serve
Slices of toast
Gherkins

Food processor

1. Place the ham shanks and pig's trotter in a large pan, and cover with fresh cold water. Bring this to the boil, skim off any impurities and add all the other ingredients apart from the parsley leaves. Simmer gently for 4 hours, then leave to cool.

2. While the shanks are cooking, make the pease pudding. To do this, rinse the soaked peas and place them in a saucepan, cover with fresh cold water and bring to the boil. Skim off any impurities and simmer until the peas are tender. Add a good pinch of salt, and continue cooking the peas until they start to break up. Drain them in a sieve and leave to cool.

3. When the peas are cool, blend them in a food processor until they're smooth. Add the vinegar and walnut oil a little at a time, pulsing the mixture in between each addition. Check the seasoning, cover and keep the pease pudding chilled until you need it.

Continued on page 60

4. When the ham is cool enough to handle, carefully remove it from the pan, along with the carrots. Strain the stock through a fine sieve into a clean pan and discard all the other ingredients. Skim off any impurities and heat the stock, reducing the volume to a syrup consistency.

5. Cut the skin, excess fat and bones away from the ham shanks, keeping the meat in good-sized chunks. Dice the cooked carrots and place them, with the ham, in a large bowl. Chop the parsley leaves and mix them in gently, and then pour the reduced syrup-like stock over the ham, carrots and parsley.

6. On a clean work surface, spread out a large triple layer of cling film. Place the ham mixture in the centre and roll it firmly into a tube shape. Tie the ends of the cling film so it resembles a sausage, then chill it overnight.

7. Remove the cling film. Carve thick slices of the terrine onto a serving plate and serve with pease pudding (which should be at room temperature), slices of toast and gherkins.

Beer Battered Fish and Chips with Mushy Peas

Fish and chips fried in beef dripping is a distinctive taste of the North East, made famous by Harry Ramsdens in Leeds and the Magpie Café in Whitby. In my version, the chips are cooked three times for extra crunch.

Serves 4 30 mins preparation, 30 mins cooking

Ingredients
4 fillets of haddock, cod, pollock or
whiting, pin-boned and skinned
1.2kg Maris Piper potatoes, peeled and
chopped into wedges
3.5kg beef dripping or 2 litres rapeseed oil
1 tablespoon sea salt
Flour to coat

For the mushy peas
250g frozen garden peas
1 teaspoon sea salt
1 teaspoon caster sugar
Small bunch mint leaves

For the beer batter
500ml beer
1 egg yolk
5g dried yeast
10ml malt vinegar
200g plain flour
Sea salt and milled black pepper

Large pan or fryer
Food thermometer

To make the beer batter
1. Combine all the batter ingredients in a bowl, and whisk together until smooth. Leave to stand for 30 minutes before you use it.

To prepare the thrice-cooked chips
1. Place the potato wedges in a bowl, and run them under cold water for a couple of minutes to rinse off the starch. Put them in a large pan and cover with water. Add a good pinch of salt, and bring them to the boil, then reduce the heat and simmer for 6-8 minutes until almost cooked. Tip them carefully into a colander and leave to dry.

2. In an electric deep fryer or large pan, heat the beef dripping or rapeseed oil to 130°C. Fry the chips in batches for 4-5 minutes, until they're lightly golden, then remove and drain on kitchen paper. When cool, keep in the fridge until you need them.

Continued on page 64

Beer Battered Fish and Chips with Mushy Peas

To make the mushy peas

1. Put the peas, salt and sugar in a saucepan, and add enough water to just cover the peas.

2. Bring the water to the boil, simmer for 3 minutes, and then add the mint leaves. Drain half of the cooking liquor into a bowl and keep to one side.

3. Using either a hand blender or food processor, pulse the peas to crush them (making them mushy) but don't over blend. You may need to add some of the liquor you've saved. Check the seasoning, and keep the peas warm until you need them.

To finish the cooking and serve

1. Heat the fryer to 190°C.

2. Coat each fillet of fish in flour and submerge in the batter. Pick each one up from the tail end, letting the excess batter run off.

3. Very carefully, lower the fish into the fryer until you eventually have to let go. Fry two fillets at a time, cooking for 6-8 minutes until golden and crispy.

4. Use a slotted spoon or tongs to remove the fish, placing it on kitchen paper and keeping warm while you finish the chips.

5. To finish the chips, fry them again in batches for 4 minutes until crisp and golden. Drain them on kitchen paper and sprinkle with a little salt.

6. Serve the fish with the chips, and the mushy peas on the side.

Roast Beef and Yorkshire Pudding

With a nice marbling of fat, fore rib stays tender while it's roasting and has loads of flavour. It's my favourite Sunday joint – and always with my light, crispy Yorkshires.

Serves 6 20 mins preparation, 2 hours 20 mins to 3 hours 40 mins cooking, 30 mins resting

Ingredients
4kg beef fore rib (ask for it French trimmed on the bone)
2 tablespoons olive oil
1 tablespoon sea salt
Milled black pepper

For the gravy
2 heaped tablespoons plain flour
500ml beef stock

For the Yorkshire pudding
115g plain flour
1 dessertspoon English mustard powder
3 eggs
275ml milk
Sea salt and milled black pepper
6 teaspoons beef dripping

Roasting tin
Yorkshire pudding tray

To cook the beef

1. Pre-heat the oven to 220°C/gas mark 7.

2. Rub olive oil all over the beef and season it with salt and pepper.

3. Heat a heavy-based roasting tin on the hob. When it's hot, add the beef and sear on all sides, then roast in the oven for 20 minutes.

4. Reduce the heat to 190°C/gas mark 5. Roast the beef for another 30 minutes per kilo for rare, or add 10 more minutes per kilo for medium or 20 more minutes per kilo for well done.

5. Once cooked, take the beef out of the oven, transfer it to a suitable dish, and cover loosely with foil. Leave to rest for 30 minutes in a warm place.

To make the gravy

1. Pour off the excess fat from the roasting tin, keeping 2 tablespoons in a small bowl. Mix this with the plain flour until you have a smooth paste. Add the stock to the roasting tin, and bring to a simmer, using a wooden spoon to loosen the baked-on pan juices. When this is boiling, whisk in the flour paste to thicken, then pour the gravy into a saucepan and continue to simmer until you're ready to serve.

Continued on page 68

Roast Beef and Yorkshire Pudding

To make the Yorkshire pudding and serve

1. Pre-heat the oven to 200°C/gas mark 6.

2. Sift the flour and mustard powder into a large bowl. Beat the eggs in a separate bowl, then add them to the flour and keep beating, gradually adding the milk. Season with salt and pepper.

3. Put a Yorkshire pudding tray – with either 12 small or 6 large cavities – into the oven to heat up, then add about 1 teaspoon of beef dripping to each cavity. Put it back in the oven for several minutes, until the fat is smoking hot.

4. Carefully remove the tray from the oven and use a ladle to pour the batter mixture into each cavity, filling each one to two thirds.

5. Return the tray to the oven for 15-20 minutes, until the puddings are well risen and golden.

6. Serve immediately with the roast beef and gravy.

North East

Singin' Hinnies

Originating in Northumberland, these fruity griddlecakes make a nice change for afternoon tea or even breakfast. And the name? Well, 'hinny' is an affectionate term in the North East, and the 'singin' is the sizzling of the butter and lard on the griddle as the cakes cook.

Makes 6-8 20 mins preparation, 20 mins cooking

Ingredients

450g plain flour
½ teaspoon table salt
¼ teaspoon bicarbonate of soda
½ teaspoon cream of tartare
120g chilled unsalted butter, diced
100g chilled lard plus extra to
grease, diced

180g mixed currants, raisins and sultanas
Zest of 1 lemon
A dash of milk

6cm cutter

1. Sift the flour, salt, bicarbonate of soda and cream of tartare into a bowl. Add the butter and lard, and rub together with your fingertips until it resembles breadcrumbs.

2. Mix in the fruit and lemon zest, then add enough milk to form a dough.

3. Roll out the dough on a lightly floured surface until it's 5mm thick. Cut out 6-8 discs, using a 6cm cutter.

4. Rub a cast iron griddle pan with a little lard, and heat it up. When it's hot, cook the hinnies in batches for 5-6 minutes on each side. Serve them warm with plenty of butter.

Singin' Hinnies

Apple Pie and Wensleydale Cheese

Apple Pie and Wensleydale Cheese

There's an old Yorkshire saying, 'Apple pie without cheese is like a kiss without a squeeze'. If you think you prefer cream or custard, try this classic combination and you may just be converted!

Serves 6-8 30 mins preparation, 1 hour cooking, 1 hour 30 mins chilling

Ingredients

For the pastry
230g plain flour
150g chilled unsalted butter, diced
Zest of 1 lemon
75g caster sugar
1 medium egg and 1 medium egg yolk, beaten together

For the filling
5 Bramley cooking apples
25g unsalted butter
150g caster sugar, plus extra to dust
3 eating apples
2 tablespoons milk

To serve
250g Farmhouse white Wensleydale cheese

20cm loose-bottomed flan tin, 5cm deep

To make the pastry

1. Place the flour and butter in a large bowl, and gently work them together until the mix resembles breadcrumbs.

2. Stir in the lemon zest and sugar, then slowly mix in the eggs to form a dough.

3. Shape the dough into a ball, wrap in cling film and keep in the fridge for 1 hour.

Continued on page 74

To make the filling

1. Peel, core and quarter the cooking apples, and slice them thinly.

2. Place the butter in a large, heavy pan over a medium heat, and let it melt. Add the cooking apples and sugar, cover with a lid and cook gently for 10-15 minutes, stirring occasionally.

3. Spread the cooked apples onto a large tray to cool.

4. Peel, core and quarter the eating apples. Slice them thinly and mix them into the cooking apples.

To make and bake the pie

1. On a floured surface, roll out two thirds of the pastry to 5mm thick. Line the flan tin with the pastry, letting it hang over the sides.

2. Put the tin on a baking tray and keep it in the fridge for another 30 minutes.

3. Place the remaining pastry between two floured sheets of baking parchment and roll to form the pie lid. Put this in the fridge for 30 minutes too.

4. Pre-heat the oven to 180°C/gas mark 4.

5. Remove the lined pastry tin from the fridge and fill it carefully with the apple mixture.

6. Brush the edges of the pastry with a little milk. Remove the parchment paper from the lid and place on top of the pie. Press gently around the edges to seal it, and trim off the excess pastry.

7. Cut two slits in the centre of the lid, brush with the remaining milk and sprinkle with the extra caster sugar.

8. Bake the pie for 50-55 minutes until it's a nice, golden colour.

9. Let it rest for 15 minutes before removing from the tin, then serve it with a slice of Wensleydale cheese.

Monachyle MHOR, Perthshire

SCOTLAND

When I think of Scotland, I think of all those foods (and drinks) where Scottish producers are considered some of the finest. Venison and other game, beef, salmon (in fact, fish and seafood of all kinds), raspberries, oats, and, of course, whisky. I've included most of them here, and thoroughly enjoyed doing it.

I also had a marvellous time visiting a genuine foodie's paradise: Monachyle MHOR Hotel, on the banks of Loch Voil in the Trossachs. This is a fantastic family business, including not just a luxury hotel, but also a fishmonger, an artisan bakery, and a 2,000-acre estate where they farm deer, sheep, cattle, pigs and hens. Not surprisingly, the food in the restaurant is strictly local, and shows what can be achieved when you have control over how your ingredients are produced, as well as cooked.

During my trip north of the border, I discovered a distinctive 'taste of Scotland'. I've tried my best to recreate this here.

SCOTLAND RECIPES

Soft-Boiled Egg with Asparagus Soldiers

Soft-Boiled Egg with Asparagus Soldiers

When local asparagus is in season, around May and June, it's so much better than anything that's travelled hundreds of food miles. This fun starter is an unusual way to serve it.

Serves 4 20 mins preparation, 5 mins cooking

Ingredients

6 slices thin streaky bacon
5 large free-range eggs
2 tablespoons milk
2 tablespoons plain flour
Sea salt and milled black pepper
4 tablespoons breadcrumbs

20 large asparagus spears
2 litres vegetable oil

Baking tray
Large pan or fryer
Food thermometer

1. Pre-heat oven to 180°C/gas mark 4.

2. Place the bacon on a non-stick baking tray, and cook in the oven for 10-15 minutes, until golden and crispy. Remove from the oven, and let it cool.

3. In a large pan of boiling water, boil 4 of the eggs for 4 minutes. Remove from the heat, and cool under a cold running tap for 2 minutes.

4. Carefully tap the eggshells all over and roll them on a work surface, then pick off the shell.

5. Whisk the remaining egg with the milk.

6. Place the flour in a small bowl and season with salt and pepper.

7. Place the cooled crispy bacon in a plastic bag and bash with a rolling pin to make bacon crumbs. In a bowl mix these with the breadcrumbs.

8. Dust each egg with flour, then dip into the egg wash and roll them in the crumbs. Repeat with the remaining eggs and keep in the fridge until you need them.

9. Trim the asparagus by snapping off the tough base of each spear and trimming with a vegetable peeler.

10. In an electric deep fryer or large pan, heat the oil to 160°C.

11. Bring a large pan of salted water to the boil, and cook the asparagus for 2-3 minutes.

12. Meanwhile, fry the eggs carefully for 3 minutes until golden, and drain on kitchen paper.

13. Slice the top off each egg just before serving and add 5 asparagus spears to each plate.

Kedgeree

Kedgeree

Believed to have been invented in Scotland in the late 18th Century, by Scottish soldiers who had previously served in India, kedgeree is a delicious blend of spicy, smoky and salty flavours. Traditionally served for breakfast, it is also lovely for lunch or supper.

Serves 4 35 mins preparation, 25 mins cooking

Ingredients

300g basmati rice
450ml vegetable stock
500g natural undyed smoked haddock fillet
350ml milk
40g unsalted butter
1 large onion, peeled and finely chopped
1 carrot, peeled and finely chopped
2 sticks celery, peeled and finely chopped

1 tablespoon medium curry powder
1 tablespoon plain flour
125ml double cream
Juice of ½ lemon
Sea salt and milled black pepper
Small bunch chives, finely chopped
3 hard-boiled eggs, peeled and quartered
1 tablespoon flat leaf parsley, chopped

1. Place the rice in a saucepan with the vegetable stock. Bring to the boil, then reduce the heat, put the lid on the pan and cook for 10 minutes.

2. Take the pan off the heat and leave the rice to finish cooking for a further 10-15 minutes, without removing the lid.

3. Meanwhile, place the haddock fillet in a large pan and pour in the milk. Bring to the boil, then take it off the heat, cover with a lid and leave for a further 5 minutes.

4. Using a slotted spoon, transfer the haddock onto a plate, keeping the milk to one side. Discard any skin and bones, and flake the fish into large chunks.

5. Melt the butter in a saucepan, add the onion, and cook for 2-3 minutes before adding the carrot and celery.

6. Cook for a further 5 minutes, then add the curry powder and flour, stirring all the time.

7. Strain the milk into the vegetable mixture, stirring vigorously as the sauce comes together. Continue cooking gently for another 10 minutes, then add the cream, lemon juice and season to taste. Stir in the haddock chunks and chives.

8. Using a fork, fluff up the rice, and turn it onto a warm dish. Pour the sauce over and fold it into the rice. Decorate the kedgeree with the quartered boiled eggs and chopped parsley.

Roast Grouse with Bread Sauce and Game Chips

Scotland is known throughout the world for its game, and grouse in particular is associated with wild northern landscapes. The birds have rich, firm meat that roasts quickly, and works perfectly with these traditional accompaniments.

Serves 4 40 mins preparation, 35 mins cooking

Ingredients
4 young grouse, dressed
Sea salt and milled black pepper
40g softened unsalted butter
½ onion, peeled and chopped
1 carrot, peeled and chopped
1 stick celery, chopped
1 sprig thyme
50ml port
100ml red wine
400ml chicken stock
1 dessertspoon redcurrant jelly

To garnish
Small bunch watercress

For the bread sauce
½ onion
1 bay leaf
3 cloves
300ml milk
4 slices stale white bread
Sea salt and milled black pepper
1 pinch nutmeg

For the game chips
2 Maris Piper potatoes
2 litres rapeseed oil
Table salt

Mandolin
Large pan or fryer
Food thermometer
Roasting tin

To make the bread sauce
1. Place the onion, bay leaf, cloves and milk in a small saucepan. Bring to the boil, then remove from the heat and leave to infuse.

2. Trim the crusts from the slices of bread and discard them. Cut the bread into small cubes.

3. Strain the infused milk into a jug, then pour it back into the pan, along with the bread. Over a low heat, gently stir the bread until it breaks down into a smooth sauce. Season with salt and pepper and a pinch of nutmeg. Keep the sauce to one side, in a warm place.

Continued on page 86

Roast Grouse with Bread Sauce and Game Chips

To make the game chips

1. Peel the potatoes and slice them very thinly using the criss-cross part of a mandolin. Wash them under a cold tap to remove as much starch as possible, then dry them on kitchen paper.

2. In an electric deep fryer or large pan, heat the oil to 190°C. Fry the potato slices for 2-3 minutes until golden brown. Season the chips with a little table salt and keep them warm.

To cook the grouse and make the gravy

1. Pre-heat the oven to 200°C/gas mark 6.

2. Season the grouse inside and out with salt and pepper, and smear it all over with the soft butter. Heat a roasting tin on the hob until it's very hot, and sear the grouse on all sides.

3. Take the tin off the heat and roast in the oven for 16-18 minutes.

4. Remove the grouse from the roasting tin and keep them warm.

5. Add the onion, carrot, celery and thyme to the tin. Cook them for a few minutes over a low heat, scraping any sediment from the bottom of the roasting tin.

6. Add the port and red wine, then increase the heat and reduce the volume by half. Add the stock, bring to the boil and simmer for 10 minutes.

To finish the dish and serve

1. Whisk the redcurrant jelly into the gravy and pass through a fine sieve into a gravy boat.

2. Reheat the bread sauce.

3. Place the grouse on warm plates, and serve with the bread sauce, gravy and a pile of game chips. Garnish with a few sprigs of watercress.

Chargrilled Haunch of Venison Forestiere

Seared on the griddle, these marinated venison steaks are bursting with flavour. Forestiere ('of the forest') is characterised by deep hearty flavours, usually including mushrooms. With the rich port-and-wine sauce, you've got a very satisfying main course.

Serves 4 1 hour 10 mins preparation, 10 mins cooking, 6 to 12 hours chilling

Ingredients
4 x 150g venison haunch steaks

For the marinade
2 tablespoons olive oil
2 bay leaves
1 sprig thyme
2 cloves garlic, thinly sliced
8 juniper berries, crushed

2 sprigs thyme
4 tablespoons olive oil
100g bacon lardons
100g button mushrooms
200ml port
250ml red wine
400ml beef or veal stock
Sea salt and milled black pepper

For the sauce
1 tablespoon sea salt
12 small shallots

To serve
Creamed mashed potatoes
(see page 36 for my recipe)

To marinade the venison
1. Put the venison steaks and all the marinade ingredients into a large freezer bag. Seal the bag and lightly massage the contents.

2. Chill in the fridge for at least 6 hours or overnight.

To make the sauce
1. Pre-heat the oven to 180°C/gas mark 4.

2. Place a large sheet of kitchen foil on a work surface. Scatter the sea salt in the centre, and lay the shallots on top. Add the sprigs of thyme and a splash of olive oil.

Continued on page 90

Chargrilled Haunch of Venison Forestiere

3. Gather the foil together to make a parcel. Place this on a baking sheet and roast in the oven for 25 minutes, until the shallots are tender. Remove from the oven and leave to cool.

4. Open the parcel and, with a sharp knife, carefully remove the skins from the shallots. Keep the shallots to one side.

5. In a hot pan fry the bacon lardons until crisp. Drain on kitchen paper and keep to one side.

6. Using the same pan, cook the mushrooms (with a little extra oil if required) for 3-4 minutes. Keep to one side.

7. Heat a saucepan over a high heat, add the port and reduce the volume by half. Then add the red wine and reduce by half again before adding the beef or veal stock.

8. Bring the sauce to the boil, then turn down the heat to a gentle simmer and cook for 15-20 minutes, reducing the volume again.

To cook the venison and serve

1. Take the venison steaks out of the fridge and let them come up to room temperature for 20 minutes.

2. Heat a griddle pan. Remove the venison steaks from the marinade, putting them on a clean plate and removing any marinade that may have stuck to them.

3. When the griddle pan is very hot, season the steaks with salt and pepper, and sear for 4-5 minutes on each side. Keep in a warm place to rest for 5 minutes.

4. Meanwhile, reheat the sauce and add the shallots, bacon lardons and mushrooms. Bring it to the boil.

5. Carve the venison steaks and place on a warm plate. Spoon over the sauce and serve with creamed mashed potatoes.

Chicken Tikka Masala

Chicken Tikka Masala

We eat this in Indian restaurants, but it's acknowledged as a British dish. The true origins are unclear, but it's reputed to have been invented in Glasgow! I like to think of it as a Scottish take on Asian cuisine – big, spicy flavours, but not too hot.

Serves 4 20 mins preparation, 35 mins cooking

Ingredients

3 tablespoons rapeseed oil
600g skinless chicken breast, cut into large pieces
1 large onion, peeled and diced
2 cloves garlic, crushed
2 red chillies, deseeded and finely sliced
2cm piece of ginger, peeled and grated
1 teaspoon chilli powder
1 teaspoon turmeric powder
2 teaspoons garam masala
1 tablespoon brown sugar
2 tablespoons tomato purée

500g very ripe tomatoes, chopped (or 1 x 400g tin chopped tomatoes)
150ml natural yoghurt
2 tablespoons coriander leaves, chopped
Juice of ½ lemon
Sea salt and milled black pepper

To serve
Steamed basmati rice

Food processor

1. In a large frying pan, heat 2 tablespoons of rapeseed oil. Add the chicken pieces and cook until lightly coloured. Keep them to one side.

2. Using the same pan, add another tablespoon of oil and the onion. Cook for 2-3 minutes until soft, stirring as you go.

3. Add the garlic, chillies and ginger to the pan, followed by the chilli powder, turmeric, garam masala and sugar. Cook for another 2 minutes.

4. Next add the tomato purée and tomatoes, and cook for 20 minutes until the tomatoes have softened.

5. Pour the sauce into a food processor and blend until smooth. Return it to the pan, add the chicken pieces, and bring back to the boil. Simmer gently for 10-15 minutes, until the chicken is cooked through.

6. Stir in the yoghurt with half the coriander. Season with the lemon juice, and salt and pepper to taste. Place the chicken tikka masala in a serving dish, scatter with the remaining coriander leaves and serve with steamed basmati rice.

Scottish Shortbread

Crumbly, buttery shortbread is the perfect partner to a cuppa. In this recipe, I've added egg yolks for extra richness, and a touch of vanilla to give these biscuits even more luxurious flavour.

Makes 16-18 biscuits 15 mins preparation, 10 mins cooking, 1 hour chilling

Ingredients
200g unsalted butter
100g icing sugar
2 drops vanilla extract
2 egg yolks
250g plain flour
1 pinch salt
1 tablespoon caster sugar

9cm round biscuit cutter
Non-stick baking sheet

1. In a large bowl, using a wooden spoon, mix the butter, icing sugar and vanilla extract until they become light and fluffy.

2. Add the egg yolks and mix until smooth.

3. Sift in the flour, mixing until it begins to combine with the other ingredients.

4. Tip the mixture onto a cool, clean, floured work surface and knead it lightly with your hands to form a dough. Wrap it in cling film and chill in the fridge for an hour.

5. Pre-heat the oven to 190°C/gas mark 5.

6. Working quickly on a cool, floured work surface, roll out the dough until it's 3mm thick. Cut into biscuits, and place them on a non-stick baking sheet. Prick them with a fork and bake for 8-10 minutes, until lightly golden.

7. Sprinkle the biscuits with caster sugar while they're still hot, and then leave to cool for 5 minutes before transferring them carefully onto a wire rack.

8. Serve immediately or store in an airtight container – they'll keep for 2-3 days.

Scotland

Scottish Shortbread

Scottish Raspberry Cranachan

Three great Scottish products – raspberries, whisky and oats – come together in this creamy, crunchy traditional dessert. We've updated it slightly, and added more interest to the texture, by including a nutty granola rather than just oats.

Serves 4 20 mins preparation, 45 mins cooking

Ingredients

200g raspberries, plus 12 to serve
500ml double cream
4 tablespoons malt whisky
4 tablespoons clear honey
150g granola (see recipe below)

20g sunflower seeds
20g pumpkin seeds
20g golden linseed
20g sesame seeds
2 heaped tablespoons clear honey
2 heaped tablespoons maple syrup
½ teaspoon ground cinnamon
1 pinch salt

For the Granola

40g pecan nuts
40g cashew nuts
40g hazelnuts
200g rolled oats

Large baking tray

To make the granola

1. Pre-heat the oven to 150°C/gas mark 2.

2. Lightly crush the pecan nuts, cashew nuts and hazelnuts.

3. In a large bowl, mix all the ingredients together.

4. Spread the mixture evenly over a large baking tray and bake for 45 minutes. Halfway through cooking, stir the granola so you end up with an even, golden colour throughout.

5. Leave it to cool, then store in an airtight container. This will make more than enough granola for this recipe and will keep for 2-3 weeks.

To make the raspberry cranachan

1. Using a fork, crush the raspberries into a rough purée.

2. Whip the double cream until it becomes stiff, then stir in the whisky and honey. Mix this well, but don't over-whip.

3. Fold in the granola and raspberry purée, until you have a ripple effect.

4. Divide the mixture between 4 serving bowls, then scatter each one with the remaining raspberries and a little more granola.

Scottish Raspberry Cranachan

The Holly Bush, Hampstead

LONDON

Over recent years, London has become recognised as one of the world's great gastronomic centres, with some truly outstanding restaurants. But the capital's culinary heritage goes back centuries, benefiting from a melting pot of cultures and the renowned markets of Smithfield, Billingsgate, and the wonderfully cosmopolitan Borough.

Not surprisingly, a huge variety of eateries has evolved – yet, surviving alongside is still the good old traditional pub. An excellent example is The Holly Bush in Hampstead, where the emphasis is on British cooking using fabulous fresh ingredients. The quality of fruit and vegetables is particularly important to the chefs here, and great produce is available from Pomona Greengrocers in Hampstead.

It's fascinating how the historic blends with the new in London – on menus as well as in the architecture and culture generally. I've chosen the recipes in this section to show how some of the city's classic dishes are still relevant, and very popular, today.

LONDON RECIPES

Omelette Arnold Bennett

Omelette Arnold Bennett

Legend has it that The Savoy Hotel created this creamy smoked haddock omelette for the novelist Arnold Bennett, who wrote an entire novel while staying there. That book was published in 1930, and this recipe has remained a classic ever since.

Serves 4 30 mins preparation, 15 mins cooking

Ingredients
250g natural undyed smoked haddock fillet
250ml milk
8 large eggs
Sea salt and milled black pepper
20g unsalted butter
50g mature Cheddar cheese, grated

4 baking dishes

For the hollandaise sauce
250g unsalted butter
50ml white wine vinegar
50ml water
Juice of ½ lemon
Sea salt and milled black pepper
3 large egg yolks
1 pinch cayenne pepper
4 tablespoons double cream, whipped

To make the hollandaise sauce

1. Clarify the butter by gently melting it in a small pan and scooping off any solids that form on the surface. Carefully ladle off the clear melted butter from the milky liquid and keep it in a warm place.

2. Put the vinegar, water, lemon juice and a pinch of salt and pepper into a small saucepan. Bring to the boil and reduce the volume until you have about 3 tablespoons. Pass the liquid through a fine sieve into a bowl.

3. Add the egg yolks to the bowl and use a whisk to mix them with the vinegar reduction. Set the bowl over a pan of simmering water, and whisk vigorously for a few minutes until the sauce is thick and creamy, and you can see a trail from the whisk in the mixture. Still whisking, slowly add the clarified butter.

4. Finally add a pinch of cayenne pepper and keep the sauce in a warm place.

To make the omelette and serve

1. Cook the haddock by placing it in a large pan with the milk and bringing it to the boil. Take it off the heat, cover with a pan lid and leave to stand for 5 minutes.

2. Using a slotted spoon, transfer the fish to a plate, draining off and discarding the milk. Flake the fish into large chunks, removing any bones and skin.

3. Divide half the fish equally between 4 individual baking dishes. Keep the other half to one side.

Continued on page 104

4. Pre-heat the grill to high.

5. Lightly whisk 3 of the eggs with a little salt and pepper.

6. Heat a non-stick frying pan over a low heat. Add half of the butter, followed by the eggs, and use a wooden spoon to scramble the eggs for a couple of minutes until they are soft and sloppy. It's important to work quickly as the eggs will continue to cook. Divide the scrambled eggs equally between the 4 dishes, spooning them over the haddock.

7. Divide the remaining haddock between the 4 dishes, placing it on top of the eggs.

8. Lightly whisk the remaining eggs and scramble them as before, and then divide them between the 4 dishes.

9. Using the back of a spoon, smooth the top of each dish, and sprinkle the grated cheese over.

10. Fold the whipped cream into the hollandaise sauce, and pour the sauce over the cheese. Smooth over the top of each dish, then glaze them under the hot grill and serve.

Salt Beef and Carrots

Salt Beef and Carrots

This dish has evolved from an old Cockney recipe, often known as 'cured beef stew'. Slow cooking brings out all the flavour of a relatively cheap cut of meat – and although it takes a few hours to cook, it's very easy to prepare.

Serves 6 20 mins preparation, 4 hours 15 mins cooking, soak overnight

Ingredients

1.5kg lean, salted beef brisket
2 onions, peeled and chopped
1 stick celery, chopped
1 leek, chopped
2 bay leaves
4 cloves
4 juniper berries
6 peppercorns
Large sprig thyme
Handful parsley stalks

18 medium carrots, peeled whole with a bit of stalk attached

To serve
Fresh peas
Mashed potatoes
English mustard

Large casserole dish or pan, suitable for the hob

1. Soak the brisket in a large bowl of water overnight. Then remove it from the water and tie it up with string to form a neat joint.

2. Place the beef in the casserole dish or pan, and cover with fresh cold water. Add the rest of the ingredients, apart from the carrots.

3. Bring the water to the boil and simmer gently for 3½ hours. Then add the carrots and cook for a further 30-35 minutes.

4. Lift the beef and carrots carefully out of the stock and onto a serving dish.

5. Pass the stock through a fine sieve into a clean pan. Skim any fat from the surface and bring the stock to the boil, reducing the volume slightly to make a gravy. Pour it into a gravy boat.

6. Serve the beef surrounded by the carrots, with the gravy, fresh peas, mashed potatoes and a pot of English mustard.

Steak and Kidney Pudding

Steak and Kidney Pudding

By the time this steamed pudding is cooked, all the meaty ingredients are melting together in a thick, dark, irresistible sauce. And well before that, the aromas from the kitchen will really get your mouth watering.

Serves 6 25 mins preparation, 4 hours cooking, 1 hour chilling

Ingredients

For the pastry
125g suet
125g soft breadcrumbs
190g plain flour
1 teaspoon salt
110ml cold water

For the filling
1kg braising steak, diced
200g veal kidneys, diced

30g plain flour
Sea salt and milled black pepper
200g onions, peeled and chopped
200g button mushrooms
1 litre beef stock
3 tablespoons Marmite
1½ tablespoons English mustard
1 dash Worcestershire sauce

2 litre pudding basin

To make the pastry

1. Mix all the dry ingredients together using a fork, then slowly add in the cold water and bind to form a dough. Wrap in cling film and chill in the fridge for an hour.

2. On a floured, cool work surface, roll out the pastry until it's 3-4mm thick. Then use two thirds to line a 2 litre pudding basin, and with the remaining one third make a disc to act as a lid.

To make the filling and cook the pudding

1. In a large bowl, mix the braising steak, veal kidneys, flour, salt and pepper. Add the onions and mushrooms, and mix everything lightly together.

2. In a separate bowl, whisk the beef stock, Marmite, mustard and Worcestershire sauce. Pour this mixture over the meat and mix thoroughly.

3. Pour the filling into the lined pudding basin. Brush the edges of the pastry lid with cold water and place it on top of the pudding, pressing down and crimping the edges to seal.

4. Place buttered greaseproof paper over the top, and then cover the pudding with a double layer of tin foil with a crease in the middle to let it expand. Tie the foil firmly onto the basin with string.

5. Steam the pudding for 4 hours, either in a steamer or by placing an upturned saucer in the base of a saucepan, half filling with boiling water and covering with a lid.

London

Scotch Eggs

The Holly Bush is renowned for its Scotch eggs, made to a traditional recipe with no fancy twists.

Makes 5 25 mins preparation, 20 mins cooking

Ingredients

7 medium free-range eggs (5 whole and 2 beaten)
450g Cumberland sausage meat
450g minced pork
2 fresh sage leaves, finely chopped
Sea salt and milled black pepper

100g plain flour
450g breadcrumbs
2 litres rapeseed oil

Large pan or fryer
Food thermometer

1. Bring a saucepan of water to the boil.

2. Place the 5 eggs in carefully, turn down the heat and simmer for 4 minutes.

3. Remove the saucepan from the heat, and wait 5 minutes before pouring off the hot water. Then run cold water over the eggs until cool.

4. Place in the fridge for 5 minutes – this makes them easier to shell.

5. Remove the shell, rinse, and keep to one side.

6. Combine the sausage meat, minced pork and sage in a bowl, mixing well until smooth. Season with pepper.

7. Divide the mixture into 5 balls and flatten them out. Place an egg at the centre of each and enclose the egg with the flattened mixture – a bit of water on your hands will prevent it from sticking.

8. In an electric deep fryer or large pan, heat the oil to 180°C.

9. Season the flour with salt and pepper.

10. Taking 1 Scotch egg at a time, coat them in the seasoned flour, then dip into the beaten eggs, and finally coat in the breadcrumbs.

11. Fry the eggs for 8-10 minutes. Drain on kitchen paper, and season with salt and pepper.

Scotch Eggs

Custard Tarts

Serves 6-8 30 mins preparation, 20 mins cooking, 10 mins cooling

Ingredients

Butter, to grease the pudding moulds or
muffin tin
200g caster sugar
100ml water
Zest of ½ lemon, peeled in wide strips
1 large cinnamon stick
½ vanilla pod, split
25g plain flour

25g cornflour
200ml whole milk
75ml double cream
3 egg yolks
1 whole egg
375g all-butter puff pastry

10 metal pudding moulds or 12-hole muffin tin

1. Lightly grease with butter 10 small, metal pudding moulds or 10 wells of a 12-hole muffin tin, and keep to one side.

2. Put the sugar in a heavy-based saucepan with the water, lemon zest, cinnamon stick and vanilla pod. Bring this slowly to the boil to make a syrup.

3. Mix the flour and cornflour in a small bowl, and stir in a splash of the milk to make a paste.

4. In a small pan, bring the remaining milk and the cream to the boil.

5. Stir the flour paste into the simmering milk mixture, whisking to prevent lumps forming. Cook until thickened.

6. Remove the lemon zest, cinnamon stick and vanilla pod from the syrup, and stir in the milk mixture, along with the egg yolks and egg. Again, whisk over the heat until it becomes thick.

7. Pour the custard into a jug, cover the surface with cling film and leave to cool.

8. Pre-heat the oven to 220°C/gas mark 7 and make sure the base of the oven is clear.

9. Roll out the pastry to form a 20cm x 30cm rectangle. Cut it in half lengthways. Lay one half on top of the other, and using your hands roll the pastry to form a long cylinder. Slice the cylinder into 10 pinwheels, each about 2cm thick.

10. Lay the pinwheels flat on a work surface and roll them out into 10cm diameter discs. Press each disc into a greased pudding mould or muffin tin well to form a 'cup'. Divide the custard between the pastry cups.

11. Bake the tarts for about 20 minutes, directly on the base of the oven, until the pastry is golden and the custard tops are coloured. Leave to cool in the tins for 10 minutes before turning out carefully. Serve warm or cool.

Custard Tarts

Chelsea Buns

Chelsea Buns

Dating from the 18th century, these fruit-filled buns were first made at the Bun House in Chelsea, a popular place for royalty as well as the general public. It was demolished long ago, but thankfully the recipe is still going strong!

Makes 12 buns 30 mins preparation, 30 mins cooking, 40 mins rising

Ingredients

500g strong bread flour
1 teaspoon fine salt
25g unsalted butter
7g yeast
2 eggs
200ml milk
50g caster sugar
2 teaspoons ground cinnamon

Zest of 1 lemon
Zest of 1 orange
50g golden raisins
50g sultanas
50g semi-dried apricots, chopped
25g unsalted butter, melted

Baking tray

1. In a large mixing bowl, rub the flour, salt and the first 25g of butter with your fingertips, until you have the consistency of fine crumbs. Stir in the yeast.

2. Warm the milk until it's just hot.

3. In a separate bowl, whisk the eggs and milk together, then pour over the crumb mixture and mix until it becomes a soft dough.

4. Turn the dough onto a lightly floured work surface and knead for 10 minutes by hand – or for 5 minutes in a mixer with a dough hook.

5. Roll the dough out into a rectangle 30cm x 25cm. Sprinkle it with the sugar, cinnamon, lemon and orange zest, and add all the dried fruit, then roll it up like a Swiss roll.

6. Cut the roll into 3cm-thick slices. Lay the slices flat on a baking tray lined with baking parchment, leaving a couple of centimetres between each one.

7. Cover the slices with lightly oiled cling film, and leave them in a warm place to double in size – this should take 30-40 minutes.

8. Pre-heat the oven to 170°C/gas mark 3.

9. Remove the cling film, and brush the buns with the melted butter. Bake for 30 minutes until golden brown. For extra sweetness, you can sprinkle a little more caster sugar on top before you serve them.

Lemon Tart

Lemon Tart

In the 1980s, the Roux brothers introduced this modern classic at Le Gavroche in London. It's still a favourite dish on their menu – and on many menus around the country.

Serves 4-6 35 mins preparation, 50 mins cooking, 1 hour chilling

Ingredients
For the pastry
250g plain flour
85g icing sugar
120g chilled unsalted butter, diced
Zest of ½ lemon
1 large egg yolk, lightly beaten
1 egg yolk to seal the pastry

For the filling
9 eggs
400g caster sugar
Zest of 2 lemons
Juice of 5 lemons
250ml double cream
50g icing sugar

25cm tart ring, 3½cm deep, greased
Baking beans or dry rice

To make the pastry
For my recipe refer to page 26.

To make the filling and finish the tart
1. Reduce the oven temperature to 130°C/gas mark ½.

2. In a bowl, whisk the eggs, caster sugar and lemon zest in a bowl until smooth. Add the lemon juice and cream, and continue to whisk until all the ingredients are thoroughly combined. Leave to stand for 5 minutes, and skim any froth from the surface.

3. Pour the filling into a jug. Place the tart case (still on the baking sheet) on the middle shelf of the oven and pour in the filling, as close to the top of the pastry as possible.

4. Bake the tart for 45-50 minutes, until it looks set. It should have a slight, even 'quiver' when you gently shake the baking sheet.

5. Leave the tart to cool to room temperature.

6. Trim off the excess pastry, remove the ring and dust the tart with icing sugar.

7. If you wish, you can caramelise the sugar under a hot grill, until it turns a light golden brown.

8. Cut the tart into slices and serve.

The Tollgate Inn, Holt

SOUTH WEST

With its gentle climate, beautiful countryside and picturesque villages, the South West has many attractions for visitors – especially those interested in food. The lush pastureland means succulent meat and magnificent dairy produce, like clotted cream and, of course, Cheddar cheese. And fruit is in abundance here: apples for eating, cooking and making cider, and soft fruit, such as blueberries.

It all adds up to a strong enthusiasm for all kinds of rich, tasty and satisfying foods – which is what I really love about The Tollgate Inn, in Holt near Bradford on Avon. With ingredients produced as close to home as possible, food miles are kept to a minimum here. Beef comes literally from 'the farm across the road' and vegetables are grown in nearby Bromham.

There's a real respect for local flavours in the South West, and I've done my best to bring them out in the recipes I've collected here. I hope you enjoy trying them.

SOUTH WEST RECIPES

Chicken and Dorset Blue Cheese Mousseline with Chive Butter Sauce

Chicken and Dorset Blue Cheese Mousseline with Chive Butter Sauce

Serves 4 30 mins preparation, 15 mins cooking

Ingredients

50g chilled unsalted butter, diced
plus a little extra to grease
200g skinless chicken breast
2 egg whites
200g blue cheese (Dorset Blue if possible)
Milled black pepper
300ml double cream

200ml fresh chicken stock
1 teaspoon lemon juice
2 heaped tablespoons chives, chopped

4 dariole moulds
Food processor
Steamer pan

1. Put the bowl of your food processor in the freezer to chill for 5 minutes.

2. Butter the dariole moulds lightly.

3. Chop the chicken breast into small pieces and place in the food processor. Blend to a smooth paste, then add the egg whites, and pulse until they're mixed in.

4. Crumble the blue cheese into the chicken mixture, then use the pulse button again to blend. Scrape down the sides and base of the bowl to make sure everything has mixed evenly, and season with a little pepper. Again using the pulse button, slowly pour in the double cream, being careful not to over blend.

5. Fill each dariole mould to the top with the mousseline, and tap them down to remove any air pockets. Lay a piece of cling film on the top of each one, and keep in the fridge until you need them – they'll keep for up to 12 hours.

6. Bring a steamer pan to the boil, place the mousselines in and steam them for 10-12 minutes until they're firm to the touch.

7. Meanwhile, heat the chicken stock in a heavy-bottomed saucepan. Bring to the boil and reduce the volume by two thirds.

8. Turn out the mousselines onto a warm plate. You may need to push your finger around the edges to loosen the top and tap the base to help remove them from the dariole moulds. You may also need to slice the top of the mousselines before you turn them out, to form a flat surface for them to stand on.

9. Bring the chicken stock back to the boil. While it's boiling, whisk in the chilled butter, a little at a time. Add the lemon juice and chives. Spoon the sauce over the mousselines and serve immediately.

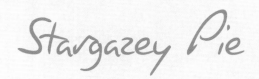

Stargazey Pie

A Cornish classic, this creamy fish, bacon and egg pie has a real 'wow' factor. Some versions have fish heads or tails sticking out of the pastry, but I've topped this one with whole langoustines.

Serves 4 40 mins preparation, 40 mins cooking

Ingredients

4 rashers streaky, rindless bacon, thinly diced
1 onion, peeled and finely chopped
150ml chicken stock
150ml fish stock
25g unsalted butter
20g plain flour
100ml white wine
200ml double cream
1 teaspoon English mustard

Sea salt and milled black pepper
2 tablespoons parsley, chopped
2 boiled eggs, shelled and chopped
6 herrings or small mackerel, filleted and pin-boned
16 shelled, fresh langoustines (plus 2 whole ones)
250g ready-made puff pastry
1 egg, beaten

Shallow pie dish

1. Heat a heavy-bottomed pan and cook the bacon until the fat turns golden. Remove from the pan and keep to one side.

2. Add the onion to the same pan, and cook for 4-5 minutes until soft. Remove and keep with the bacon.

3. Heat the chicken and fish stock together, bringing to the boil.

4. In a second heavy-bottomed pan, melt the butter and stir in the flour to make a roux, then cook for 3-4 minutes. Stirring over a low heat, add the white wine followed by a ladle of stock, and mix well until smooth before adding the next ladle of stock. When you've added all the stock, reduce the heat and cook the sauce for 10 minutes.

5. Add the cream, bring the sauce back to the boil and simmer gently until it's reduced to a nice, thick consistency. Remove it from the heat.

6. Whisk the mustard into the sauce and check the seasoning, adding salt and pepper if necessary.

7. Gently fold the cooked onions, bacon, parsley and egg into the sauce. Leave to cool.

8. Pre-heat the oven to 200°C/gas mark 6.

9. In a shallow pie dish, arrange the fish fillets and the shelled langoustines. Season with a little salt and pepper, and pour the sauce over the top.

10. Roll out the puff pastry and lay it over the dish. Trim the edges, make 2 small incisions in the top and push a whole langoustine, tail first, into each slit, leaving the head and claws above the pastry.

11. Brush the pastry with the beaten egg, and bake the pie for 35-40 minutes until it's golden and bubbling.

Beef Wellington with Red Wine Gravy

Beef Wellington with Red Wine Gravy

Lewis Rapson of The Tollgate Inn has developed this flavoursome version of a classic entertaining dish. Tender fillet beef, with a rich mushroom pâté, all wrapped up in a chive pancake and puff pastry – a really tasty way to impress your friends!

Serves 2 20 mins preparation, 30 mins cooking

Ingredients
A little oil to fry
2 fillet steaks, 6-8oz each
Sea salt and milled black pepper
100g mushrooms, chopped
100g red onion, peeled and chopped
2 eggs
50g plain flour
50ml milk
Handful of chives, chopped
300g ready-made puff pastry
Egg to glaze the pastry

For the gravy
300ml water
300ml good red wine
3 sprigs of thyme
3 sprigs of rosemary
1 beef stock cube
Sea salt and milled black pepper

To serve
Creamed mashed potatoes
(see page 36 for my recipe)

Food processor

1. Heat a frying pan, add a little oil and fry the fillet steaks for 1 minute on each side. Remove from the pan, and season generously with salt and pepper. Let them rest for at least 5 minutes (this will release any excess blood).

2. In the same pan, add the mushrooms and onion and season with salt and pepper. Fry for 5-7 minutes until soft.

3. Place the cooked mushrooms and onion in a food processor, and blitz to form a pâté. Put this to one side to cool. (Don't wash the pan – it's full of flavour, and we'll use it for our gravy.)

4. Make 2 pancakes by mixing the eggs into the flour, and then adding the milk. Whisk to remove the lumps, season well and add the chopped chives. Pour half of this mixture into a hot non-stick pan, fry for 1 minute, and then flip the pancake and cook for another minute. Transfer it to a plate to cool. Repeat this process for the second pancake.

Continued on page 128

5. Roll out the puff pastry to 2mm thick, then, using a standard-size side plate, cut 2 discs. (Keep the remaining pastry – if you fancy being creative, you could use it to decorate the top of the Wellingtons.)

6. Pre-heat the oven to 200°C/gas mark 6.

7. Place each pancake on top of each pastry disc and cut to the same size as the pastry. Then place a heaped tablespoon of the mushroom mix in the centre of each pancake and put each fillet steak on top of that.

8. Bring the sides of the pastry up and over each steak to meet all round. Then flip the Wellingtons over and use your fingertips to tuck in the bottom of the pastry so they each resemble a ball.

9. Place the Wellingtons on greaseproof paper, and brush with egg. If you've made any pastry decoration, place this on top and brush again.

10. Cook the Wellingtons in the oven for 12-15 minutes for rare, or 15-18 minutes for medium. Let them rest before serving.

To make the gravy

1. In the pan used for the beef and mushrooms, add the water, red wine, thyme and rosemary.

2. Boil this to reduce the volume by half, then whisk in the stock cube and reduce it further to a gravy consistency. Season to taste. Pass the gravy through a sieve to remove the thyme and rosemary.

To serve

1. Place the Wellingtons in the centre of 2 plates and pour the gravy over. Serve with creamed mashed potatoes.

Farmhouse Cheddar and Asparagus Tart

Serves 6 30 mins preparation, 1 hour cooking, 10 mins chilling

Ingredients

For the pastry
50g chilled unsalted butter, diced
50g lard or solid vegetable oil, diced
175g plain flour
1 egg yolk
4 tablespoons cold water
1 pinch table salt

For the filling
1kg asparagus
250ml milk
4 eggs
250ml double cream
Sea salt and milled black pepper
300g Mature Farmhouse Cheddar, grated

Food processor
23cm loose-bottomed quiche tin
Baking beans
Ice cubes

To make the pastry

1. Pre-heat the oven to 190°C/gas mark 5.

2. Put the pastry ingredients in a food processor and pulse until the mixture binds together. (Or you could use your fingertips to rub the butter and lard lightly through the flour until the mixture resembles breadcrumbs, and then add enough of the water to bind the pastry together.)

3. Turn the pastry out onto a lightly floured board, gather it into a ball and roll out until it's 3mm thick. Line the quiche tin with the pastry and chill in the fridge for 10 minutes.

4. Cover the pastry with greaseproof paper, put the baking beans on top, and bake for 12 minutes. Then carefully remove the baking beans and greaseproof paper, and bake the pastry for a further 5 minutes.

To make the filling and finish the tart

1. Trim the asparagus, discarding the woody ends, then cook in boiling salted water for 2-3 minutes until just tender. Transfer carefully from the hot water to a bowl of iced water. When cool, drain on kitchen paper.

2. Cut the asparagus spears in half. Keeping the tips to one side, place the remaining asparagus ends in a processor, add enough of the milk to cover them. Blend until you have a very smooth purée then pass through a fine sieve into a bowl.

3. Add the remaining milk, eggs and cream, and beat until smooth. Season with salt and pepper, mix in the cheese, and pour the mixture into the tart case. Arrange the asparagus tips attractively on top.

4. Carefully place the tart in the oven and bake for 40 minutes until it's golden brown. Leave for 5-10 minutes to cool and set before you serve.

Farmhouse Cheddar and Asparagus Tart

Fillet of Silver Hake, Crushed Potatoes, Cornish Crab and Falmouth Bay Mussels

Fillet of Silver Hake, Crushed Potatoes, Cornish Crab and Falmouth Bay Mussels

Often referred to simply as 'hake', silver hake is a mild, white, flaky fish that makes an ideal base for the stronger seafood flavours in this recipe.

Serves 4 30 mins preparation, 20 mins cooking

Ingredients

400g fresh mussels, cleaned and de-bearded
100ml white wine
2 cloves garlic, finely chopped
2 shallots, finely chopped
2 tablespoons olive oil
20g unsalted butter
4 x 175g silver hake fillet portions
200g cooked new potatoes

50ml double cream
3 tablespoons parsley, chopped
Sea salt and milled black pepper
1 lemon
100g fresh white crabmeat

Oven proof tray

1. Heat a heavy pan. When hot, add the mussels, white wine, garlic and shallots. Cover with a lid and steam for 4-5 minutes until the mussel shells open.

2. Strain the mussels through a colander over a bowl. When they're cool enough to handle, pick them out of their shells and keep them to one side.

3. Discard the shells, but keep any shallot and garlic. Put these, with the mussel broth, in a heavy pan and keep to one side.

4. Pre-heat the oven to 150°C/gas mark 2.

5. Heat a large frying pan, and add the olive oil and butter. When the butter starts to froth, add the hake fillets, skin side down, and cook for 5-6 minutes until the skin is slightly golden and crisp. Flip them over and cook for a further 4 minutes. Transfer them to a flat ovenproof tray, and put them in the oven for 5 minutes.

6. Add the cooked potatoes to the pan the fish was cooked in, and gently reheat them. Use a fork to crush them lightly (you may need to add extra olive oil, depending on the juices left in the pan).

7. While you're reheating the potatoes, place the mussel broth on a high heat, add the cream and reduce it to a thin sauce.

8. Add half of the parsley to the lightly crushed potatoes, and mix them together. Season with a little salt, and place a pile in the centre of each of the 4 warmed serving plates.

9. Place the hake fillets on top of the potatoes.

10. Add the picked mussels to the sauce and bring to the boil. Add a squeeze of lemon juice, the crabmeat and remaining parsley. Bring it back to the boil, give it a good stir, and pour it around the fish to serve.

Baked Lemon Cheesecake with Blueberries

Baked Lemon Cheesecake with Blueberries

The South West is the biggest harvesting area for English blueberries, and their slightly tart sweetness is the perfect match for this creamy lemon cheesecake. The colours look amazing too!

Serves 8-10 20 mins preparation, 1 hour cooking, 2 hours resting, chill overnight

Ingredients
85g unsalted butter, plus 5g extra to grease
160g digestive biscuits
1 tablespoon caster sugar

22-24cm springform cake tin, 5-6cm deep
Deep-sided roasting tin

For the filling
4 eggs
160g caster sugar
600g cream cheese
280ml sour cream
3 unwaxed lemons, juice and grated zest
250g blueberries
3 tablespoons water

To make the base
1. Pre-heat the oven to 150°C/gas mark 2.

2. Grease the cake tin with 5g of butter and line the base with greaseproof paper.

3. Crush the digestive biscuits, either in a food processor or in a plastic bag using a rolling pin.

4. Melt the 85g of butter, then stir in the crushed biscuits and sugar, and press the mixture into the base of the tin. Bake for 8 minutes, and then set it aside to cool.

To make the filling
1. Reduce the oven temperature to 140°C/gas mark 1.

2. Whisk the eggs lightly in a large bowl, add the sugar, cream cheese, sour cream, lemon juice and zest. Stir until the mixture is smooth and pour it over the biscuit base.

3. Wrap 2 sheets of tin foil around the outside of the cake tin, and place in the roasting tin. Pour boiling water into the roasting tin to half way up the cake tin. Bake in the oven for 1 hour.

4. Turn off the heat and leave the cheesecake in the oven for a further 2 hours. Remove from the oven and chill in the fridge overnight.

To cook the blueberries and serve
1. Place the blueberries and 3 tablespoons of water in a small saucepan. Cook for 5-6 minutes until the blueberries start popping. Leave to cool, and serve with slices of cheesecake.

Somerset Apple Cake

In an area renowned for its apple orchards and cider making, this moist, slightly spicy cake is a natural favourite. I like it best as a pudding, served warm with plenty of cream.

Serves 10-12 15 mins preparation, 1 hour cooking

Ingredients

150g sultanas
150ml cider
180g unsalted butter
225g caster sugar
2 large eggs, beaten
280g plain flour
1 teaspoon ground cinnamon
1 teaspoon mixed spice
1½ teaspoons baking powder

Zest of 1 lemon
450g large cooking apples, peeled, cored and finely chopped

To serve
Double or clotted cream

18cm round cake tin

1. Pre-heat the oven to 170°C/gas mark 3.

2. Grease and line the cake tin with greaseproof paper.

3. In a small glass bowl, soak the sultanas in the cider.

4. In a separate bowl, mix the butter and sugar together in a bowl until they become pale and fluffy.

5. Add the eggs gradually, beating well after each addition.

6. Add the flour, cinnamon, mixed spice and baking powder, and mix well.

7. Fold in the lemon zest, apples, sultanas and cider.

8. Pour the mixture into the prepared tin and bake for 1 hour, until the cake is risen and golden brown. Put the cake onto a wire rack to cool.

9. Serve while it's still warm, with double or clotted cream.

Somerset Apple Cake

The George in Rye, East Sussex

SOUTH EAST

Kent, Sussex and Hampshire enjoy some of England's kindest weather, so it's no surprise to find excellent food in these counties. Fruit and vegetables grow in abundance, and meat and cheese also feature strongly in my recipes from this region.

But probably the greatest ingredients of the South East are the fresh fish and seafood caught off this coast. As well as Dover sole, there's sea bass, mackerel, plaice, scallops and lobsters, among others, and they all find their way onto local menus, like at The George in the historic East Sussex town of Rye. With Karen Davenport at front of house, head chef Craig Wales fast-cooks seafood on a wood-charcoal grill. He needs to know it's the freshest available, which is why he buys from PH Fish of Hastings, who land catches every day from their own boat.

The culinary inspiration of this area also includes garlic from the Isle of Wight and watercress from around Chichester. So you can see how it would be difficult not to create some memorable dishes!

SOUTH EAST RECIPES

Chichester Watercress Soup

The land around Chichester is a major watercress-growing area, and here we have a tasty way to make the most of this highly nutritious 'superfood'.

Serves 4 15 mins preparation, 10 mins cooking

Ingredients
25g unsalted butter
½ small onion, peeled and diced
100g spinach leaves, washed
400g watercress, washed and with stalks removed
350ml boiling water
½ teaspoon sea salt
Milled black pepper
350g ice cubes
4 dessertspoons crème fraîche

1. Melt the butter in a large saucepan over a low heat. Add the onion and cook it gently for 3-4 minutes, until it softens.

2. Turn up the heat. Add the spinach and watercress to the pan and cook for 2 minutes, until it wilts.

3. Add the boiling water, salt and pepper, and boil for a further 2 minutes.

4. Remove the pan from the heat and add the ice cubes immediately to stop any further cooking.

5. Purée the soup in a blender until it's smooth, then reheat in a pan and serve with a swirl of crème fraîche.

Chichester Watercress Soup

Seared Scallops with Cauliflower Purée and Vegetables à la Grecque

Seared Scallops with Cauliflower Purée and Vegetables à la Grecque

At The George in Rye, seafood is served wonderfully fresh. Scallops are a particular favourite, and this recipe makes the most of their delicate sweetness.

Serves 4 30 mins preparation, 35 mins cooking

Ingredients

1 large cauliflower
300ml milk
300ml double cream
50g unsalted butter
Sea salt and milled black pepper
2 carrots, diced
2 leeks, diced
2 tablespoons white wine vinegar
Juice of 1 lemon
100ml olive oil, plus extra to fry

4 tablespoons white truffle oil, plus extra
to serve
1 bunch thyme
1 garlic clove
2 teaspoons coriander seeds, cracked
2 pinches saffron
1 clove
1 sprig rosemary
250ml dry white wine
8 large scallops

1. Cut the cauliflower in half. Slice one half thinly and put the slices in a shallow pan with the milk and cream, cover the pan and cook for 8-10 minutes or until the cauliflower is soft.

2. Remove the cauliflower from the pan and place in a food processor. Add the butter, and blend until very smooth, adding a little of the cooking milk and cream if needed to thin the purée down slightly. Pass through a fine sieve and season with salt and pepper.

3. Break the remaining cauliflower into small florets. Blanch in a large pan of salted boiling water for 3 minutes, then plunge immediately into cold water. Do the same with the carrots and leeks. Drain and place in a bowl.

4. Put the vinegar, lemon juice, oils, thyme, garlic, coriander seeds, saffron, clove, rosemary and wine in a saucepan, and bring them to the boil. Pour this over the vegetables and leave to cool completely, then remove the garlic, thyme and rosemary.

5. Heat a little olive oil in a non-stick frying pan. Add the scallops and cook for 1-2 minutes on one side. Turn them over, and cook for another minute or until they're golden and seared.

6. Place a few spoonfuls of the cauliflower purée on 4 serving plates, and smooth over to create a smear of purée. Arrange 2 scallops on each plate.

7. Drain the vegetables from the marinade and divide them between the plates. Finish with a little truffle oil.

Twice Baked Ashmore Cheese Soufflés

Twice Baked Ashmore Cheese Soufflés

Serves 6 40 mins preparation, 50 mins cooking

Ingredients

125g unsalted butter
30g dried breadcrumbs
450ml full-fat milk
½ onion, peeled and diced
1 bay leaf
2 cloves
75g plain flour
1 heaped tablespoon Pommery or
Dijon mustard
250g Ashmore or mature Cheddar
cheese, grated
6 eggs, separated

½ teaspoon sea salt
100ml double cream

To serve
Mixed salad leaves
1 eating apple, cut into matchstick pieces
at the last minute
2 tablespoons walnut oil

6 ramekin dishes
Deep sided roasting tin

1. Heavily grease 6 ramekin dishes with 50g of the butter. Dust with the breadcrumbs and chill in the fridge.

2. Place the milk, onion, bay leaf and cloves in a saucepan, and bring to the boil. Remove from the heat and let the flavours infuse.

3. Melt the remaining butter in a heavy-bottomed saucepan, stir in the flour and cook for 5 minutes, forming a roux.

4. Strain the infused milk. Add it to the roux, 1 ladle at a time, stirring continuously letting the mixture boil between each addition. When you've added all the milk, cook the mixture for a further 10 minutes on a low heat.

5. Remove the pan from the heat, and stir in the mustard and grated cheese. When the mixture is smooth, add the egg yolks, 2 at a time. Cover the pan with cling film and keep in a warm place.

6. Pre-heat the oven to 135°C/gas mark 1.

7. Whisk the egg whites until they begin to thicken. Add the salt and continue whisking until they become firm.

8. Using a wire whisk, beat half of the egg whites into the cheese mixture, then carefully fold in the rest. Divide the mixture between the ramekins and place them in a deep roasting tin. Pour boiling water around them and bake in the oven for 25 minutes.

9. Remove the ramekins from the oven and let them cool for 15 minutes or longer.

10. Increase the oven temperature to 190°C/gas mark 5.

11. Carefully turn out the soufflés onto a greased, ovenproof dish, leaving plenty of space between them, and pour the double cream over them. Bake the soufflés for 10-12 minutes until they turn golden and double in size.

12. Serve immediately with crisp salad leaves, apple matchsticks and a drizzle of walnut oil.

Roast Hampshire Pork with Apple Stuffing

Roast Hampshire Pork with Apple Stuffing

Hampshire pork is relatively lean, but there's still enough fat for great flavour – and this recipe gives you some lovely crispy crackling. All in all, it's a sumptuous roast, and the zesty apple stuffing balances the richness perfectly.

Serves 8 20 mins preparation, 1 hour 10 mins cooking, 1 hour standing

Ingredients

200ml milk
200g day-old white bread rolls, thinly sliced
60g unsalted butter
1 large onion, peeled and diced
4 Granny Smith apples, peeled, cored and diced

2 tablespoons fresh sage leaves, chopped
Sea salt and milled black pepper
2kg rack of Hampshire pork (ask for it French trimmed)
1 dessertspoon sea salt
300ml chicken stock

To make the stuffing

1. Heat the milk in a small saucepan.

2. Place the bread slices in a bowl and pour the warm milk over. Leave to stand.

3. Heat another saucepan, add the butter and onion, and cook until the onion is soft and golden. Add the apples and sage, and cook for another 2-3 minutes.

4. Using your hands, lightly squeeze the bread to remove any excess milk, and add the bread to the apples and onion. Season with a little salt and pepper, and mix lightly.

To cook and serve the pork

1. Score the rind if your butcher hasn't already done so. Then run a knife carefully from the top of the piece of pork to about half way, and pull the meat apart. Spread in the stuffing, and then close the meat up and tie it with butcher's string. Rub the skin with sea salt and leave to stand for an hour.

2. Heat the oven to 220°C/gas mark 7. Place the pork on a roasting tin and roast for 20 minutes. Reduce the heat to 180°C/gas mark 4 and continue cooking for a further 50 minutes.

3. Remove the pork from the oven, lift out of the roasting tin, and let it rest in a warm place for 15 minutes before carving.

4. Meanwhile, pour off and discard excess fat from the roasting tin. Add the chicken stock and bring it to the boil. Use a wooden spoon to remove any thickened pan juices. Simmer for 5-10 minutes to produce a light, flavoursome gravy.

5. Remove the crackling from the rack of pork and keep to one side. Discard any excess fat. Carve the stuffed meat into slices, and serve with the crackling.

Dover Sole with Brown Butter, Lemon, Capers and Parsley

Delicate in flavour but with a firm texture, Dover sole is best served simply – as in this classic regional recipe.

Serves 2 10 mins preparation, 20 mins cooking

Ingredients

50g plain flour
Sea salt and milled black pepper
2 tablespoons rapeseed oil
50g unsalted butter
2 Dover sole, 500g each – ask your fishmonger to gut them and remove the head, tail and skin

40g flaked almonds
Juice of 1 lemon
40g capers
1 tablespoon chopped parsley

1. Season the flour with a little salt and pepper.

2. Heat a large non-stick frying pan, then add the oil and 10g of the butter. When this is foaming, cover each Dover sole in the seasoned flour, and place carefully in the pan. Shake the pan gently to prevent the fish from sticking.

3. Leave the fish to cook undisturbed for 5 minutes until golden, then flip them over and cook for a further 4 minutes. Transfer them carefully from the pan onto warm serving plates.

4. Discard any oil left in the pan, and return to the heat. Let it get hot again and add the remaining butter. Let the butter foam and turn slightly nut-brown in colour, then add the almonds immediately, followed by the lemon juice, capers and parsley.

5. Spoon the butter over the Dover sole and serve.

Dover Sole with Brown Butter, Lemon, Capers and Parsley

Chicken Kiev

Using fresh garlic makes all the difference to Chicken Kiev. The Isle of Wight is a major garlic-producing area for the UK, so I like to think of it as a recipe of the South East.

Serves 4 30 mins preparation, 12-15 mins cooking, 1 hour chilling

Ingredients
4 x 175g skinless chicken breasts
½ lemon, juice and grated zest
150g softened unsalted butter
4 garlic cloves, finely chopped
2 tablespoons parsley, chopped
1 dessertspoon tarragon, chopped
Sea salt and milled black pepper
4 tablespoons plain flour
2 eggs, beaten

150g panko (or dried) breadcrumbs
Sunflower oil for frying

To serve
Thrice cooked chips (see page 62 for my recipe)
Lemon quarters
Watercress salad

Large pan or fryer
Food thermometer

1. Remove the small fillet from the underside of one of the chicken breasts, and place it between two sheets of cling film. Gently flatten it using the base of a saucepan, until you have an even, flattened fillet that has doubled in size. Repeat this with the other 3 fillets.

2. Taking the main part of the chicken breasts, cut a slit lengthways along the underside of each one with a very sharp knife. Start at the centre and cut a ¼ of the length of the breast in each direction. Then carefully cut away a little to the sides to form a pocket, making sure you don't cut right through the breast.

3. Mix the lemon juice with the butter, garlic, parsley and tarragon, and season with a little salt and pepper. Once this mixture has bound together, divide it between the 4 chicken breasts, placing it in each cut-out pocket. Bring the sides back together to seal them, and then place a flattened chicken fillet over the top of each opening. Press gently together to seal, and put them in the fridge for 15 minutes.

4. Using shallow bowls, place the flour in the first, beaten egg in the second and breadcrumbs and lemon zest in a third.

5. Taking 1 chicken breast, dip it in the flour so it's evenly covered, and shake off any excess. Then dip it in the egg and then the breadcrumbs. Gently pat it all over and shake off any excess crumbs. Then dip it in the egg again, followed by the breadcrumbs.

6. Repeat this process with the remaining chicken breasts. Place on a tray and chill in the fridge for at least an hour.

7. Pre-heat the oven to 140°C/gas mark 1.

8. Heat an electric deep fryer to 160°C and fry 2 of the chicken breasts for 8-10 minutes until golden. Drain on kitchen paper, put them on an oven tray and keep warm in the oven while you cook the remaining 2 breasts.

9. Serve with thrice cooked chips, lemon quarters and fresh watercress salad.

Chicken Kiev

English Wine Syllabub

English Wine Syllabub

This creamy, boozy dessert dates back to Tudor times. It's quintessentially English, which is why we suggest using an English sweet wine. If you can't find one in the supermarket, ask your local wine merchant – and look for 'late harvest' on the label.

Serves 6 20 mins preparation, 2-3 hours chilling

Ingredients
1 lemon
1 lime
200ml late harvest (sweet) English wine
2 tablespoons cognac
1-2 tablespoons caster sugar
(depending on the sweetness of the wine)
275ml double cream

Chilled glasses
Mixing bowl

1. Peel the zest from the lemon and lime using a peeler, then scrape away and discard any white pith. Chop the peel finely, and place in a stainless steel pan with the wine, cognac and juice from the lemon and lime. Bring to a simmer.

2. Take a teaspoon and taste to check if you need to add any of the caster sugar – remember you'll be adding a lot of cream, which will reduce the sweetness. Add some or all of the sugar as necessary.

3. Simmer for 5 minutes, then remove the pan from the heat and leave the liquid to infuse and cool completely. Cover with cling film and chill in the fridge for 1-2 hours. Also chill 6 wine glasses and a mixing bowl.

4. Pour the cream into the chilled bowl and stir in the infused wine. Using a large balloon whisk, whisk the mixture until it's loosely thick and just holding its shape.

5. Pour the mixture carefully into the chilled glasses, and return them to the fridge for 30 minutes. Eat the syllabub on the day you make it, before it separates.

Mr Underhill's, Ludlow

WALES & WEST

A land of wild mountains and welcoming valleys, Wales gives us some wonderful food. Welsh lamb, reared in some of the world's greenest pastures, is renowned for its sweet flavour. And the leeks that go so well with it have been elevated from a favourite vegetable to the country's emblem. I've used both these ingredients, and more, in the recipes in this section – as well as recreating some Welsh culinary traditions, like Bara Brith and, of course, Welsh Rarebit.

Just over the border, the West of England shares this lively food heritage. In Shropshire, the thriving market town of Ludlow has become famous for its food – from butchers' shops and farmers' markets to a number of outstanding restaurants. One of these is Mr Underhill's, a Michelin-starred restaurant with rooms, just outside the town in Dinham Weir. Here, chef Chris Bradley makes the most of local delights, such as great dairy produce and fruit, and the excellent meat and charcuterie available from Wenlock Edge Farm.

I love the enthusiasm for quality in this part of Britain – as you'll see over the next few pages.

WALES & WEST RECIPES

Shepherd's Pie

Lamb is the meat we associate with Welsh cooking, and this simple supper dish is an easy way to enjoy its distinctive flavour. There are many variations on the recipe, but I prefer this classic version.

Serves 4 15 mins preparation, 55 mins cooking

Ingredients

900g potatoes
50g butter
1 tablespoon olive oil
1 large onion, finely chopped
3 large carrots, finely chopped
450g lean minced lamb

300ml chicken stock (hot)
1 tablespoon fresh thyme, chopped
1 teaspoon tomato purée
Sea salt and milled black pepper

Gratin dish

1. Pre-heat the oven to 180°C/gas mark 4.

2. Peel, cut and boil the potatoes until soft, and then mash them with the butter.

3. While the potatoes are cooking, heat the olive oil in a large pan. Add the onion and cook gently for a few minutes, then add the carrots. Cook on a low heat for 5 minutes.

4. Add the mince and cook until coloured, using a spoon to break up any lumps.

5. Add the hot chicken stock, thyme and tomato purée, and simmer this without a lid for around 35 minutes to reduce the liquid. Keep checking to make sure it doesn't become too dry, and season with salt and pepper to taste.

6. Spread the mince into a gratin dish and cover it with the mashed potato.

7. Cook the pie in the oven for around 20 minutes until it's golden on top and hot in the centre.

Shepherd's Pie

Welsh Rarebit

Interestingly, over the centuries there have been recipes for 'Scotch rarebit' and 'English rarebit', but it's the Welsh version that survives today. With the addition of mustard and beer, it's an extra-tasty way to do cheese on toast – perfect for lunch or supper.

Serves 4 15 mins preparation, 5 mins cooking

Ingredients

50g unsalted butter
50g plain flour
200ml milk
350g mature Cheddar cheese, grated
20g English mustard
85ml beer (any type of beer will work)

3-4 drops Worcestershire sauce
Sea salt and milled black pepper
4 slices white bread

To serve
Chutney

1. Pre-heat the grill to high.

2. Melt the butter in a small saucepan, stir in the flour to make a roux, and cook gently for 5 minutes.

3. In a second pan, heat the milk to boiling point. Add a ladle at a time to the roux mixture, stirring until it's smooth between each addition.

4. Over a gentle heat, add the cheese, mustard, beer and Worcestershire sauce, and stir until the cheese has melted. Take it off the heat, and season with salt and pepper.

5. Toast the bread until it's lightly coloured, spread the rarebit mixture on top, and grill until golden.

6. Serve it just as it is, or with chutney.

Beetroot and Goats' Curd Salad

Beetroot and Goats' Curd Salad

Goats' curd is like a very soft, light, creamy goats' cheese. If you can't find it, a young, fresh goats' cheese will do – what you're looking for is that gentle tang that works so well with the sweetness of beetroot.

Serves 4 1 hour 30 mins preparation

Ingredients
2 golden beetroot
2 red beetroot
2 candied beetroot
2 tablespoons sea salt
6 sprigs thyme
2 garlic cloves
600g caster sugar
700ml malt vinegar
300g goats' curd or soft goats' cheese
1 small bag mixed salad leaves
2 tablespoons mixed nuts, toasted (optional)

Roasting tray
Food processor

For the dressing
20ml white wine vinegar
300g grated Parmesan
30g pine nuts, toasted
1 tablespoon Dijon mustard
Juice of ½ lemon
50ml rapeseed oil
50ml olive oil
40g parsley
20g basil
20g chives, chopped
20g picked tarragon leaves
Sea salt and milled black pepper

1. Pre-heat the oven to 180°C/gas mark 4.

2. Wash all the beetroot.

3. Sprinkle 2 tablespoons of sea salt on a small roasting tray. Place the golden beetroot on top and scatter with 4 sprigs of thyme, cover with kitchen foil, sealing it around the sides of the tray. Roast for 30-40 minutes until tender (pierce it with a sharp knife to check this, as the cooking time depends on the size of the beetroot).

4. In a saucepan, place the red beetroot, garlic and remaining thyme, along with 400g of sugar, 500ml of malt vinegar and 500ml or more of water to cover the beetroot. Bring this to the boil and simmer gently for 30-40 minutes, until tender.

5. When both types of beetroot are cooked, leave them to cool to room temperature. Peel them and keep to one side.

Continued on page 166

6. Peel the candied beetroot, and slice it as thinly as possible, using a mandolin if you have one. Mix the remaining 200ml of vinegar and 200g of sugar with 200ml of water. Add the sliced beetroot and marinade for 15 minutes.

7. Place all the dressing ingredients in a food processor and pulse into a smooth dressing.

To assemble the dish

1. Drain the candied beetroot, and arrange it in a fanned circle in the centre of each of the 4 plates.

2. Cut the red and golden beetroot into quarters. Stand 2 quarters of each (opposite each other) on top of the fan, keeping a small space for the salad in the centre and gaps for the goats' curd in between.

3. Using a dessertspoon, place a spoonful of goats' curd or cheese in between each quarter of beetroot. Place a few mixed leaves in the centre, sprinkle with toasted mixed nuts (if you're using them), and drizzle the dressing over and around each plate.

Chicken and Leek Pie

A national emblem of Wales, the leek is used extensively in the country's cooking. Its mild, onion-like flavour seasons this creamy chicken pie perfectly.

Serves 4 50 mins preparation, 1 hour cooking

Ingredients

500g chicken legs or thighs
½ onion, peeled and roughly chopped
1 carrot, peeled and roughly chopped
1 stick celery, roughly chopped
1 bay leaf
250ml milk
30g unsalted butter
50g plain flour plus extra to dust

100ml double cream
Sea salt and milled black pepper
2 leeks
1 tablespoon rapeseed oil
300g ready-made puff pastry
1 egg, beaten

Pie dish

1. Place the chicken, onion, carrot, celery and bay leaf in a large pan. Cover with cold water and bring to a simmer.

2. Skim any impurities from the surface and reduce the heat. Cover with a pan lid and cook gently for 40 minutes.

3. Take the pan off the heat and leave until the chicken is cool enough to handle.

4. Lift the chicken from the stock onto a plate. Skim any fats from the surface and pass the stock through a fine sieve then return it to the pan. Place over a high heat and reduce the volume by one third.

5. Discard the skin and bones from the chicken, leaving good-sized pieces of meat. Keep these to one side.

6. Pre-heat the oven to 180°C/gas mark 4.

7. In a saucepan, heat 250ml of the chicken stock with the milk. Bring to a simmer and keep warm.

8. In a second saucepan, melt the butter, then add the flour and use a wooden spoon to stir it vigorously to form a roux. Continue cooking the roux for a further 2 minutes.

9. Keep stirring while you add the milk and stock mixture, a little at a time.

10. When all the liquid is mixed in, cook the sauce on a low heat for a further 10 minutes, stirring regularly. Then remove it from the heat, add the double cream and season with salt and pepper. Leave to cool.

Continued on page 170

Chicken and Leek Pie

11. Wash the leeks under a running tap. Cut them in half lengthways, then in half again before chopping them finely.

12. Heat a frying pan, and add the rapeseed oil and chopped leeks. Cook for 5 minutes and add to the white sauce. Fold in the chicken pieces and pour the mixture into a pie dish.

13. On a floured work surface, roll out the puff pastry until it's 3mm thick, ensuring it's more than large enough to cover the dish.

14. Take a thin strip of the pastry and place it around the edge of the pie dish. Brush this with some of the beaten egg and place the pastry lid over the pie. Seal the edges by pressing them firmly together.

15. Make 3 incisions in the centre of the pastry, using scissors. Brush with the remaining egg, and bake the pie for 20-25 minutes.

Bara Brith

Bara Brith

Welsh for 'speckled bread', Bara Brith is like a cross between a traditional tea bread and a rich, sticky fruitcake. Try it for a change for afternoon tea – with plenty of butter.

Makes 1 loaf (8-10 slices) 15 mins preparation plus overnight soaking, 1 hour 20 mins cooking, 15 mins cooling

Ingredients

3 Earl Grey teabags
350ml boiling water
100g sultanas
100g raisins
100g currants
25g mixed peel
180g soft brown sugar
130g self-raising flour
100g wholemeal flour

1 teaspoon baking powder
1 teaspoon mixed spice
½ teaspoon ground cinnamon
1 large egg, beaten
1 teaspoon vegetable oil

900g/2lb loaf tin, lined with
greaseproof paper

1. In a large bowl, brew the Earl Grey tea with the boiling water. Add the dried fruit and peel, cover with cling film and leave to soak overnight.

2. Pre-heat the oven to 170°C/gas mark 3.

3. In another large bowl, mix together the sugar, both types of flour, baking powder, mixed spice and cinnamon.

4. Remove the teabags from the soaked fruit. Drain the fruit through a sieve over a bowl, keeping the liquid.

5. Add the fruit to the flour mixture, along with the beaten egg, and mix well to a thick consistency. You may need to add a little of the liquid you've saved.

6. Pour the mixture into the lined loaf tin and bake for 1 hour 20 minutes. To check the loaf is cooked, insert a skewer into the middle. If it comes out clean, it's ready.

7. Leave the Bara Brith to cool for 15 minutes before tipping it out of the loaf tin onto a wire rack. Serve it sliced and buttered – it's best eaten on the day you make it.

Chocolate Mousse

Chocolate Mousse

During my time in Wales I discovered many artisan chocolate suppliers, which inspired this rich, dark chocolate mousse. This recipe uses lots of whisked egg whites to create an especially light texture.

Serves 6 25 mins preparation, 2 to 3 hours chilling

Ingredients
250g good quality dark chocolate
(minimum 70%), broken into pieces
40g unsalted butter
6 eggs
2 drops vanilla extract
2 egg whites
40g golden caster sugar
Extra bar of chocolate for shavings

6 dessert dishes

1. Place the chocolate pieces in a heatproof bowl over a pan of simmering water. Let the chocolate melt, stir in the butter and remove the pan from the heat.

2. Separate the 6 eggs, then whisk the yolks with the vanilla extract until they're smooth.

3. Use a clean whisk to whisk the 8 egg whites until they become frothy. Add half of the sugar and whisk again until the mixture starts to stiffen. Add the remaining sugar and whisk again to form stiff peaks. Fold in the egg yolk mixture.

4. Carefully stir half of the egg mixture into the chocolate, until you have a smooth consistency. Then fold in the rest, again until it's smooth.

5. Place the mousse in 6 dessert dishes and leave to chill in the fridge for 2-3 hours.

6. To make the shavings, use a potato peeler to peel along the edge of the chocolate bar. Sprinkle the shavings over the mousse to serve.

Creamy Rice Pudding

Creamy Rice Pudding

This recipe from Mr Underhill's is a luxurious cross between rice pudding and crème brûlée. It's especially good served still warm from the grill.

Serves 6 10 mins preparation, 20 mins cooking, 2 hours chilling

Ingredients
650g double cream
600g semi-skimmed milk
100g caster sugar
1 vanilla pod
1 small pinch salt
100g pudding rice
6 egg yolks
75g caster sugar for caramelising

Large heatproof dish

1. Put 500g of the cream and all the milk in a heavy pan. Add the caster sugar, a third of the vanilla pod and a small pinch of salt. Put on a low heat.

2. Wash the rice and sprinkle into the pan. Stir until it starts bubbling, then simmer for 20 minutes, stirring occasionally. Keep to one side.

3. Whisk the egg yolks with the remaining 150g of cream. Add this mixture to the rice pan, reheating it gently. When you see the first bubble appear, remove the pan from the heat and pour the rice pudding into a cold bowl, stirring occasionally until it's cool.

4. Pour the pudding into a large heatproof dish, and chill for 2 hours.

5. To serve, sprinkle the dish with a layer of caster sugar and caramelise under a hot grill.

With thanks to...

I couldn't have completed this book without the help of some inspirational people: the chefs at the inns and restaurants I visited around Britain, and the 'food champions' who supply their superb ingredients. My profound thanks to them all. And if you'd like to check them out yourself (I strongly recommend it!) here's where you can find them.

EAST ANGLIA

The Bull at Great Totham, 2 Maldon Road, Great Totham, Essex CM9 8NH, Tel: 01621 893385, www.thebullatgreattotham.co.uk
Cressing Rare Breed Meat Company Ltd, Cressing Park, Braintree Road, Cressing, Braintree, Essex CM77 8JB, Tel: 01376 341594

NORTH WEST

The Punch Bowl Inn, Crosthwaite, Lyth Valley, Cumbria LA8 8HR, Tel: 01539 568237, www.the-punchbowl.co.uk
Udale Speciality Foods, 1-3 Schola Green Lane, Morecombe LA4 5QT, Tel: 01524 411611

NORTH EAST

The Oak Tree Inn, Hutton Magna, County Durham DL11 7HH, Tel: 01833 627371, www.theoaktreehutton.co.uk
Martin Walker, Jacksons, Hutton Magna, County Durham DL11 7HH, Tel: 01833 627577

SCOTLAND

Monachyle MHOR Hotel, Balquhidder, Lochearnhead, Perthshire FK19 8PQ, Tel: 01877 384622, www.mhor.net

LONDON

The Holly Bush, 22 Holly Mount, London NW3 6SG, Tel: 020 7435 2892, www.hollybushhampstead.co.uk
Pomona Greengrocers, 179 Haverstock Hill, Hampstead, London NW3 4QS, Tel: 020 7916 2676

SOUTH WEST

The Tollgate Inn, Ham Green, Holt, Nr. Bradford upon Avon, Wiltshire BA14 6PX, Tel: 01225 782 326, www.tollgateinn.co.uk
Church Farm Meats, Church Farm, The Street, Broughton Gifford, Melksham, Wiltshire SN12 8PR, Tel: 01225 783467, www.churchfarmmeats.co.uk

SOUTH EAST

The George in Rye, 98 High Street, Rye, East Sussex TN31 7JT, Tel: 01797 222114, www.thegeorgeinrye.com
PH Fish, 3-4 Rock-A-Nore Road, Hastings, TN34 3DW, Tel: 01424 444971

WALES & WEST

Mr Underhill's, Dinham Weir, Ludlow, Shropshire SY8 1EH, Tel: 01584 874431, www.mr-underhills.co.uk
Wenlock Edge Farm, Wenlock Edge, Shropshire TF13 6DJ, Tel: 01694 771893, www.wenlockedgefarm.co.uk

Lamona Appliance, Sink and Tap Collection

The Lamona range is exclusive to Howdens Joinery and has been selected to perfectly complement our range of kitchens.

Lamona appliances are designed to look great and are manufactured to the highest standards to ensure they are durable and reliable, use less energy and water, and run quietly, whilst providing excellent value for money.

You can choose from ovens, microwaves, hobs, extractors, fridges, freezers, dishwashers, tumble dryers, sinks and taps, which are all designed to fit beautifully in your Howdens kitchen.

All Lamona appliances come with a 2 year manufacturer's guarantee and a 5 year guarantee on oven door glass, and what we believe is the best after sales service in the UK.

You will have the reassurance that we supply 500,000 appliances and 600,000 sinks and taps each year to UK homes.

Lamona is available from stock in over 530 local depots to your trade professional. To find out more and for detailed product specifications, please refer to **www.lamona.co.uk**

Burford Cream Kitchen

Lamona Round Bowl Sink with Drainer and Lamona Chrome
Orta Swan Neck Monobloc Tap

Lamona Built-Under Double Fan Oven and Lamona Professional Gas Hob

The General Tarleton

An old coaching inn with contemporary comforts, The General Tarleton Inn is in the pretty village of Ferrensby close to both York and Harrogate. Owned and run by John and Claire Topham for the past 14 years, The General Tarleton is constantly evolving but always sticks to the basic philosophy of offering great service and excellent food and drink in a relaxed atmosphere, and if you are staying the night, a comfortable room to rest your head.

The focus is on food

In The General Tarleton kitchen, John heads an experienced and dedicated team. Menus change daily to reflect the seasons and the pick of the catch or crop that day. John gets a call most days from the fishing boats as they return to port and within hours the fish is in the kitchen. Yorkshire has an abundance of excellent suppliers which The General Tarleton has worked with over the years to obtain the very best seasonal produce.

The General Tarleton Inn, Boroughbridge Road, Ferrensby, Knaresborough, HG5 0PZ
Tel 01423 340284 www.generaltarleton.co.uk